Smithsburg - 1875
Courtesy of Smithsburg Historical Society

D1306352

THE

POETICAL WORKS

of

Edgar Irving Brenner

PRINTED BY
BEIDEL PRINTING HOUSE, INC.
SHIPPENSBURG, PENNSYLVANIA

Copyright © 1990 by the Smithsburg Historical Society

All rights reserved — no part of this book may be reproduced in any form without permission in writing from the publisher, except by a reviewer who wishes to quote brief passages in connection with a review.

Printed by
Beidel Printing House, Inc.
63 West Burd Street
Shippensburg, PA 17257

In respect to the scholarship contained herein, the acid-free paper used in this book meets the guidelines for permanence and durability of the Committee on Production Guidelines for Book Longevity of the Council on Library Resources.

ISBN 0-932751-07-5

PRINTED IN THE UNITED STATES OF AMERICA

Dedication Sonnet

In Memory of Edgar Irving Brenner

Thy life was brief, We will not say too brief —
Such thoughts are born of doubt and unbelief.
We cannot tell why God bade thee depart.
No mortal eye can pierce the dismal gloom
With which He chooses to enshroud the tomb.
But shining marks oft times attract death's dart.
Thy God hath called thee from this vale of grief
With him to dwell, because thou'rt "pure in heart."
We thought to love thee long, But as the flower
Begins to fade before it's bloomed an hour,
Or as the glories of the western sky
Grow dim ere scarce their splendors reach the eye,
So hast thou passed so soon from earth away,
To serve thy God in realms of endless day.

— Rev. Norman Plass

ACKNOWLEDGMENTS

The Smithsburg Historical Society is grateful to Florence Jacques Hager who made the manuscripts of Edgar Irving Brenner available as well as family photographs; to Florence Brenner Sitler who edited and collated Edgar's manuscripts in 1935; to the Smithsburg Branch of the Myersville Bank for its generous support; to Linda Shillinger for donating her time and proofreading talents; to Gettysburg College for their assistance in researching Edgar's college years and donation of photographs; to the Yale University Library for their support in providing photographs; to Professor Charles H. Glatfelter of the Adams County (Pa.) Historical Society for his advice and photograph of Gettysburg; to Mary Ferranti of the New Haven Colony Historical Society for the photograph of Lake Whitney; and to all those members of the Society who worked so diligently to bring Edgar Irving Brenner's works to the public.

TABLE OF CONTENTS

⊰{ POEMS }⊱

POEMS *continued*

⊸{ MADRIGALS }⊷

MADRIGALS *continued*

⊰ BALLADES AND RONDEAUS ⊱

⊰ SONNETS ⊱

⊸{ Swan Song }⊷

⊸{ Dated Poems }⊷

⚜ MISCELLANEA ⚜

MISCELLANEA *continued*

INTRODUCTION

The Life And Times
Of Edgar Irving Brenner

Edgar Irving Brenner - 1882
Photo Courtesy of the Brenner Family

More than 125 years ago, Edgar Irving Brenner was born in the quiet, rural farming community of Smithsburg, Maryland. Nestled in the shadow of South Mountain, the town of Smithsburg bustled with commerce supporting the rich orchards and fields in this region of the Cumberland Valley. Edgar was one of nine Brenner children brought into the world by Lucien and Catherine Brenner. Lucien was a leading businessman and merchant in Smithsburg.

Edgar grew up in this peaceful community, virtually untouched by the Civil War battles that raged in nearby Gettysburg and Antietam. He attended Smithsburg public schools where he was active in school plays, especially as an orator. His life changed markedly in December 1881 when Lucien and Catherine sent him off to Pennsylvania College in Gettysburg at the young age of sixteen.

Edgar excelled at Pennsylvania College (now known as Gettysburg College). His scholarly achievements were unparalleled. In those years, there were 139 undergraduate students at Gettysburg and it rivaled Dickinson and Franklin and Marshall as a fine and selective college. Students from 29 different states were in attendance. In 1881 it was an all male college, although a debate raged over the possible admission of women. Women were eventually admitted in 1884 and the transition went smoothly, much to the pleasure of the male student body. By January 1882, Edward was elected to the prestigious Phrena Literary Society. Later that year, he was elected as recording secretary and in 1885 was elected president. The Phrena Society was one of two literary and debating societies at Gettysburg, the other being the Philo Society. Edgar participated regularly in debates.

Edgar was noticed and admired by the editor of the *Pennsylvania College Monthly*, a prominent literary magazine with nationwide distribution. Its editor was Professor Phillip M. Bikle, also a native son of Smithsburg and a well-known professor at

Catherine Fiery Brenner - Mother
Photo Courtesy of the Brenner Family

Lucien B. Brenner — Father
Photo Courtesy of the Brenner Family

Gettysburg College between 1874 and 1934. Professor Bikle wrote of Edgar's literary debates. At the same time Professor Bikle published a number of beautiful poems in the *Pennsylvania College Monthly* under the pseudonym "Diogenes Blank, Jr.," a mysterious author who chose to conceal his identity.

The young man from the small village of Smithsburg grew in stature at Gettysburg, culminating in his graduation in 1885 at the young age of 19 as valedictorian and with the highest honors of his class. He was a member and enthusiastic leader of the Phi Kappa Psi social fraternity. During his years at Gettysburg he decided on a career as a professor of English and literature. Sometime during the summer of 1885, Edgar decided to seek a degree from the prestigious Yale Divinity School where he was accepted into the freshman class of 1885. He excelled at Yale as well. In 1886, one Professor Harris described Edgar as the brightest man at the seminary though he was only 21 years of age and in his second year.

Then tragedy struck at Yale. Lake Whitney, the resort for all New Haven ice skaters, claimed the life of Edgar Irving Brenner. Dispatches from Yale, Smithsburg and *The Baltimore Sun* told the story. Edgar and his classmate, Charles Loomis, were skating on Lake Whitney in the afternoon of December 21, 1886. The ice on the lower lake was firm, but Edgar and Charles skated some two miles toward the upper reaches of the lake. They did not realize that currents upstream kept the ice thin. Edgar shot ahead of Charles and, before he could react, fell through the ice into the frigid waters. In spite of Edgar's warning cries, Charles skated toward him to try to pull him out. Instead of succeeding, Charles also fell through. A farmer, who was driving over a nearby bridge, saw the accident, unbuckled the reins from his horses and threw a strap to Charles, but the strap broke. At the same time a small boy who had skated toward the hole also fell in. Another boy pulled him out with a hockey stick while the farmer again threw the straps toward Charles and this time pulled him out. But by this time Edgar had disappeared beneath the ice. Two hours later an eddy brought his body to the surface nearly at the same spot where he had fallen through the ice.

December 28, 1886 was a chilly gray day in Smithsburg. The burial of perhaps Smithsburg's most brilliant son cast a shadow over the village and a pale over the usual holiday festivities. Edgar's death, at the threshold of such a promising career, seemed particularly incomprehensible. Reverend C. Dorsy Hoover, who graduated from Yale the previous spring, journeyed to the small Cumberland Valley town to take charge of the remains and assist the Brenner family. He read a series of resolutions adopted by Edgar's Yale classmates mourning their loss and the "inscrutable dispensation and over-ruling providence of the Heavenly Father who removed Edgar Irving Brenner, their classmate."

This might have been a forgotten, but sad, incident in the history of the Brenner family and the village of Smithsburg had it not been for a recent discovery, the manuscripts of the brilliant and youthful Edgar Irving Brenner. What has been left unsaid to this point in this introduction is that Edgar was not only a brilliant, popular scholar and leader, but he was also an incredibly prolific and sensitive literary writer and a poet of no small measure. He wrote more than one hundred and fifty poems, many of which were published, in his short literary life between his years at Gettysburg and his untimely death at Yale. And he sometimes published under the pseudonym of "Diogenes Blank, Jr.," the mysterious poet from Smithsburg, Maryland. This volume presents the poetry of Edgar Brenner.

The original manuscripts were held by the Brenner family for more than a hundred years. They were brought to light when a member of the family mentioned them to the members of the newly-formed Smithsburg Historical Society. Society members read the beautiful, romantic and prophetic verses and jointly decided that they were not only beautiful, but merited publishing for all to see. With the splendid cooperation of the Brenner family, we have endeavored to present not a selected few, but all of the known works of Edgar Brenner. Many of these works were widely published in the last century in notable magazines and journals such as *The Detroit Press, The Weekly Sun, The Chicago Current, The New York World* and *The New York Graphic.* We now understand that he was engaged to regularly furnish poetry to a New York paper and was about to publish a volume of his poems when Lake Whitney interrupted his plans.

We believe that Edgar Irving Brenner's poetry is timeless. He wrote verses of love, sadness, old friends, of Maryland, and of Gettysburg after the end of the Civil War. Had he lived a full life, we believe this remarkable American poet and writer's works would have become loved throughout the land. The poetry in this volume was written by the time Edgar was but 21 years of age. His insight and maturity are rare for his years. The Smithsburg Historical Society and the Brenner family are pleased to present Edgar Irving Brenner's masterpieces.

The Smithsburg Historical Society — 1990

POEMS OF
EDGAR IRVING BRENNER
COMPILED BY
FLORENCE BRENNER SITLER

1935

In Varied Strain
by
Edgar Brenner

"--Overmastered by some thoughts,
I yielded an inky tribute
unto them"--

Sir P. Sidney--"The Defense of Poesy."

Rondeau Dedicatory--
To
Joseph Baker Hileman, Jr.

In varied strain our hopes we penned
In days that are no more, old friend,
When brooks and flowers and misty mile
Served all our doubts to reconcile,
In that long Spring-time, now at end.

Life pays a sorry dividend;
The years their annual message send,
And sing us both of trust and wile
In varied strain.

Would that these random rhymes could lend
More worth this boldness to defend;
But if thine old-time friendly smile
Shall greet my modest pages, I'll
Let all the world despise, commend,
In varied strain.

3

The Eve Before The Wedding

Why, Joe, dear old boy, is that you?
Sit down and let's try to be jolly.
I've been feeling confoundedly blue - -
So you're on your way down to see Polly?

Cigar? These are good. Here's a light.
(I'm afraid it's a vice past repressing.)
Draw up to the fire. A cool night;
And a fire (with a friend) 's a rare blessing.

How've you been since the ball? - - I'm at sea
To know what I'll do when you're married.
Tomorrow's the day; - - and to me
It seems all my hopes have miscarried.

You know we had planned a snug den,
Which we two together should dwell in;
Where, released from the boredom of men,
We'd escape, too, each troublesome Helen.

"L'homme propose" - - Don't quote it. I know,
" 'Tis love makes the world go" at college
We sang. I suppose it is so;
But, you know, I can't speak from knowledge.

"Get a wife for myself?" Heavens! Joe,
I should have to look up my profession.
I am destined to hoe the old row
Past any attempt at progression.

Hard luck this, old fellow. You smile,
Forgive my nonsensical chatter.
I said "Let's be jolly" - - the while
I've been grumbling. I truly don't flatter.

Not going? Oh, Polly expects you,
And you won't disappoint her. You're right.

4

("My secret there's no one suspects".) You
Are happy. God bless you. Good-night!

(After Joe's departure.)
God bless him, dear fellow, but more
God bless his sweet wife. May he prove her
True husband.

****And now shut the door
On vain dreamings.****
--God! How I love her!

*Published in "N.Y. World" Oct. 31, 1886;
also "San Francisco Post," and "Philadelphia Press."*

My Lady's Glove

My lady's glove! The dainty tips
I softly pressed unto my lips,
And cavalierly bended knee,
As if, her Knight, I would but see
What will of hers 'twere mine to do.
I dared not utter all my love,
"Ah me!" I thought, "if she but knew--"
And kissed my lady's glove.

She read the thought, "Sir knight, arise!"
I met her dewy, dark-blue eyes
And saw the love-light there. My sweet,
Need words such hallowed love repeat?
I kissed my lady's lips. Command
She gave me not my faith to prove.
Blest day! When I shall own the hand
That wore my lady's glove.

*Published in "N.Y. Graphic" of December 4, 1885;
and in "Chicago Current" November 28, 1885.*

5

At The Window

As, with soft sighs, she lifted her white hand
To soothe her aching head that fain would rest,
A jasmine-tree, that o'er the casement spanned,
Kissed her fair hair and nestled at her breast.
Starting, she smiled to be so well-caressed,
And kissed the flower as 'twere a magic wand,
As, with soft sighs, she lifted her white hand
To soothe her aching head, that fain would rest.

Then grew her pale face happy, as she scanned
The rosy-tinted promise of the West.
"When comes my dear love for his own," she planned,
"These jasmine-flowers shall greet him first and best."
As, with soft sighs, she lifted her white hand
To soothe her aching head that fain would rest.

Published in "Every Other Saturday" December 19, 1885.

In Maryland

In Maryland the warm winds sweep
As soft as baby-breaths that creep
From baby-lips in smiling sleep.
From Eastern shore of Chesapeake
To where the Alleghanies stand
'Tis fair. No fairer land I seek.
Stern North takes on a sudden freak
And woos sweet South's consorting hand--
In Maryland.

Across Potomac's volumed line
Virginia's sister-features shine
From out a labyrinth of pine;
And broad-browed Pennsylvania towers

6

Above, by harsher breezes fanned;
While East, along Atlantic's strand
        Sits Delaware.

    Earth nowhere showers
A wreath of sweetlier-bosomed flowers,
    Or fairer maidens, sunnier hours,
    Or nobler men to win command;
    And gladder music nowhere pours
Than from the lute touched full and bland
        In Maryland.

    The flowering vistas seem to float
    A softened music, rich and rare,
Like shepherd strains on pipe of oat.
    The trees wave idly in the air,
        A graceful retinue of green
        To yonder lightly-tripping queen,
    The fairest of all Maryland's fair.
    She flits along the orchard-close,
    And love goes with her as she goes,
    With blossoms dropping on her hair.
    Her eyes are laughing as the sight,
    Her cheeks are rosing with the breeze,
    Her heart is leaping with delight,
    Her limbs are graceful as the trees,
        And all about her birds and bees
        Are making merry with a might
    Befitting her, Pomona's daughter.
--Ah! From near by the glistening water,
    That quivers through the tinted mesh
        Of rugged bole and lacing bough,
There comes a song, full clear and fresh,
    That calls glad flushes to her brow;
And back her answering love-song floats,
    A very radiance of notes.

7

The birds sang wondrously that day,
But, tell me, have you ever heard
A song - - that was a song - - of bird
That sang not love? And so for aye
'Tis "love, love, love" - - love found, love sought,
Love lost - - yet love. - -
Ah, what fond hopes were fondly planned
In Maryland!

Still through the orchard as of old
The sunlight lingeringly falls,
And peeps by shaded orchard walls
At moss-grown seats where love was told,
Along the shores of Chesapeake
The golden waters lap and lave,
The wind still sighs across the wave,
A lover on his lady's cheek;
And still freaks on the dancing brook
Through many a secret, bosky nook.

- - 'Tis well. The hopeful heart she gave
Was buried with him in his grave.
Still fair she is and sweet, but, oh!
At times the sweet face saddens so!
But life has gained an added strength
For all the care her years have spanned.
And o'er its breadth and down its length,
Where'er its dances, like flowers, expand,
No nobler heart, no life more grand
In Maryland!

Published in "The Weekly Sun" July 24, 1886.

Her Letter

A small, sweet-scented square of white,
An artless, artful, witching sight,
　　Her letter lies.
I know what lurks behind the seal,
And yet, somehow, I seem to feel
As if each letter must reveal
　　Some glad surprise.

I pause to think just when she wrote;
The office, date and stamp I note,
　　And stiff address.
If I should judge from these prim lines
How much of sweetness it enshrines,
I'd never find me colder signs,
　　I must confess.

But well her bonny hand I know
No other message could bestow
　　Than tender only.
Mayhap she wrote in that old nook,
Where oft in quiet hours she took
Some magazine or recent book,
　　And cheered me lonely.

These lines her little hand ran o'er;
Her dream-blue eyes ran on before;
　　And here, I think,
She kissed the letter thrice for me.
Dear little girl of mine, I see
Her sweet face bending lovingly,
　　So softly pink.

Well, well! I break the seal at last.
No thinking of a happy Past
　　Makes Present better.
I read the words of love within ----

9

Some day another man will win,
(A younger, better paladin)
Just such a letter.

Here's to his health. My friends, fill up
Of wine one glowing, sparkling cup,
Or, crystal water;
May this dear girl her pure heart plight
To one whose virtues got him hight
"A verray parfit gentil knight"--
For she's my daughter.

Published in "Detroit Free Press" July 1886

Impromptu

"Afflatus divine" can't you come,
Can't you give me some rest from this longing
Which possesses my fingers and thumb
And impels me to rhyme which is thronging
My whole being through, and its gonging
A noise in my head like a drum,
Can't you give me some rest from this longing,
"Afflatus divine," won't you come?
I say it is mean and you're wronging
A spirit that ever is dumb
To all common ills. O, what gonging--
Say, spirit divine won't you come,
Can't you give me some rest from this longing
That came from the extra dry Mumm?

* * * * * * * * * * * * * *

When cares afflict you, then, my friend, don't worry,
But hold a jolly mirror to their gaze
And when they see in that their faces sorry
They'll turn to other quarters in amaze.

*-- written one evening in college when Mose and I had just
returned from somewhere -- I don't exactly remember --*

10

Give Me The Old

Old wine to drink, old wood to burn, old books
to read, and old friends to converse with.

Old wine to drink! --
Ay, give the slippery juice,
That drippeth from the grape thrown loose
Within the tun;
Plucked from beneath the cliff
Of sunny-sided Teneriffe,
And ripened 'neath the blink
Of India's sun!
Peat whiskey hot,
Tempered with well-boiled water!
These make the long night shorter, --
Forgetting not
Good stout old English porter.

Old wood to burn! --
Ay, bring the hill-side beech
From where the owlets meet and screech,
And ravens croak;
The crackling pine, and cedar sweet;
Bring too a clump of fragrant peat,
Dug 'neath the fern;
The knotted oak,
A faggot, too, perhap,
Whose bright flame, dancing, winking,
Shall light us at our drinking;
While the oozing sap
Shall make sweet music to our thinking.

Old books to read! --
Ay, bring these nodes of wit,
The brazen-clasped, the vellum-writ,
Time-honored tomes!
The same my sire scanned before,
The same my grandsire thumbed o'er,

The same his sire from college bore,
The well-earned mood
Of Oxford's domes:--
Old Homer blind,
Old Horace, rake Anacreon, by
Old Tully, Plautus, Terence lie;
Mort Arthur's olden minstrelsie,
Quaint Burton, quainter Spenser, ay,
And Gervase Markham's venerie,--
Nor leave behind
The Holy Book by which we live and die.

Old friends to talk!--
Ay, bring those chosen few,
The wise, the courtly and the true,
So rarely found;
Him for my wine, him for my stud,
Him for my casel, distich, bud
In mountain walk!
Bring Walter good, With soulful Fred; and learned Will,
And thee, my alter ego, dearer still
For every mood.

Chance

A blushing rose, as summer days withdrew,
Drooped, by degrees, its gentle, queenly head;
And when its beauty vanished, life went, too--
The rose was dead.

A charm from off a radiant Hebe face
Fled with the years. Both youth and joy were gone;
But goodness left a higher beauty's grace,
And love lived on.

Published in Chicago "Current" December 5, 1885.

Cecilia

When last Cecilia leaned her hand
Upon the trellis by my door,
Her cheek the light wind found and fanned,
Her slender shadow crossed the floor.

She lingered in the golden light,
With calm eyes looking sweetly down,
And spoke of wrong and spoke of right,
And went her way toward the town.

'Twas but a moment ere she went,
Yet still I see her standing there,
A simple, sweet embodiment
Of youth and hope and all that's fair.

I know not if she thought it much
To cheer me by her words that day,
But all my future felt the touch
And influence of Cecilia.

I sorrow that she came no more
To learn the wonder she had wrought,
But through the rose-enclustered door
No shadow of her have I caught;

But once as fleets each quicker year,
When roses bloom by every way,
The birds of summer gather near,
And help me keep Cecilia's day.

A Dedication

(To my old college friends.)

For you, glad company,
That, free from care, a-lying
Face upward in the vale of Life, to see
What clouds o'ercast our sun of Verity, - -
And then, too quickly dazzled by his light,
Closed eyes and smiled, but never thought of flight
Nor cared what winds were flying; - -

For you, old friends and true,
(Truer as older growing),
Though now that pleasant vale is changing hue,
Its rocks more rugged and its skies less blue,
Yet wisdom gives us strengthened sight to scan;
We look for Truth; and for the good of man
We learn the good of Knowing; - -

For you, ye scattered set,
(I've lingered long in writing) - -
I hang this wreath in Memory's cabinet.
God grant ye good; and let your joy be met
In knowing in the after-time of Life
That strife for Truth, when nobly fought, is strife
That Love makes all-uniting.

January 16, 1885
Pennsylvania College - - Room 42
8:30 P.M.

Pennsylvania College - circa 1885
Photo Courtesy of the Special Collections, Gettysburg College

To Her I Sing

As, in a web a spider weaves,
Hold fast, a diamond raindrop gleams,
Though shaken by the impetuous streams
And dimmed by shadows of the leaves,
Outflashes all its wealth of beams,

So, in the web of all my song,
Thy sweetness, O my love, is held,
And though the web be soon excelled
By better weavers of the throng,
The sweetness gleams unparallelled.

Or rather, while my web I weave,
Thy sweetness beats it through like rain;
And, though it beat and beat again,
It cannot simply come and leave;
--Some captured pearls will still remain.

Published in the Chicago "Current" September 4, 1886.

A Retrospection

My darling, when your hair was brown,
The bloom was fresher on your cheek,
You were the fairest of the town.

In spite of old-maid Wisdom's frown,
I laughed at each enchanting freak,
My darling, when your hair was brown.

The love that sighed my mad-cap down
Brought deeper charm with every week,
You were the fairest of the town.

One night you wore a witching gown,
And pride for love was all too weak,
My darling, when your hair was brown.

16

And one bright morn a bridal crown
Adorned a woman, pure and meek,
You were the fairest of the town.

A sweeter bride the "good Haroun"
Forever and a day could seek
For, darling, when your hair was brown,
You were the fairest of the town.

Published in "N.Y. World" December 12, 1886.

* * * * * * * * * * * * * * *

My darling, now your hair is gray
Your life-long love has made me blessed
You still are fairer than the day.

Young love makes merry while it may
Old love our lives have taught is best
My darling now your hair is gray.

Though down this peace and pain starred way
Full far our trusty feet have pressed
You still are fairer than the day.

Who shall a true wife's glory say
Who just requite her faithful breast
My darling now your hair is gray.

The bloom that faded fades for aye
Love writes an endless palimpsest
You still are fairer than the day.

Forever though my feet may stray
My happy heart shall this attest
My darling, now your hair is gray
You still are fairer than the day.

April 17, 1886

Her Love Was True

"Well, well, the wisest bond to Fate.
My brown old books around me wait,
My pipe still holds, unconfiscate,
Its wonted station.
Pass me the wine. To those that keep
The bachelor's secluded sleep,
Peaceful, inviolate and deep,
I pour libation"--Austin Dobson.

Her love was true long years ago
In soft June evenings' after-glow,
And thought I, as I stroked her hair,
If love had ever been so fair,
Or sweeter face did angels know.

She seemed so frank; the gentle flow
Of all her words came sweetly slow;--
She told me once she'd <u>really</u> <u>swear</u>
Her love was true.

Dear me! How very far below
The Past's horizon do I go!
Mutannur nos; and, ah! ma chere,
The years have burdened us with care.
----I found 'twas to some other beau
Her love was true.

Published under pseudonym Diogenes Blank, Jr.

O Silver Cloud

O silver cloud, a moment, white
Thou gleamest fair within my sight,
Then off beyond the mountain's blue
I lose thee in the darkening hue
Of comrade-clouds whose ranks unite.

Art thou a snow-clad neophyte,
Attendant on the Queen of night,
Hurrying to join her retinue,
O silver cloud?

Mayhap, O truant, by her might
Eos demands thy service-right
To bind her golden locks, or woo
Her rosy face to smile anew, --
Or dost thou follow Phoebus' flight,
O silver cloud?

Published in Chicago "Current" December 26, 1885.

Lines In A Waiting-Room

"The more fool he!" -- I turned to know
What sweet-voiced maiden thought him so; --
To meet a rosy face, an air
Of saucy sweetness nestling there.
-- He must have been a fool, I trow.

I wonder if that sudden glow
Is still upon her. Apropos,
I'll look again. I re-declare
The more fool he!

Is he a tall and whiskered beau?
Is he a friend? Mayhap, a foe?
I wonder how and when and where
And why such sweet disdain he'd dare?
-- I cannot tell. I'm certain, though,
The more fool he.

Published in N.Y. "World" January 20, 1886.

19

Phantasmagoria

Oh! 'twas in a forest wild,
 Far away,
Sweetest visions past me filed,
 Day by day.
Time was slow and Life was joy,
 It was Ease without alloy,
Cupid, mischief-working boy,
 Stayed away.

On a verdant bank I sat,
 In a dream.
Through the flower-studded plat,
 Trilled a stream.
Clouds of gorgeous-colored light,
 Fading slowly out of sight,
Showed me Phoebus in his might,
 With his team.

As I sat there, "fancy-free,"
 In that bower.
Came a vision jauntily.
 From a flower.
Growing large and larger still,
 It developed at my will, - -
Caused my very soul to thrill,
 With its power.

Radiant eyes and golden hair
 Made me wild,
Lips, divine beyond compare,
 On me smiled.
Up I sprang and clasped her tight,
Held her close with all my might,
 In a super-mad delight,
 So beguiled.

20

Rained I kisses on her lips,
Ere she spoke,
As the bee sweet honey sips,
Thus I broke
Every vow 'gainst Love I'd made;
For this goddess there I prayed - -
Then - - "Get up," my chummy brayed,
And - - I woke.

Manuscript lost; copied from published poem signed by Diogenes Blank, Jr.

Golden-Rod

Tell, O yellow Golden-rod
Tell me, tell me whether,
As you swayed upon her breast,
Resting-place the downiest
You or yours have ever pressed,
O'er the fields of heather,
Did her heart beat high for me
As we walked together?

She was very kind and sweet,
She is always so.
Do you think she meant to be
Any kinder then to me
Just because she felt that she
Wanted to, you know?
Tell me, did you feel her heart
Beating fast or slow?

Why I love her, Golden-rod,
Once I tried to tell,
But my reasons fled away
Like the stars before the day
When she came upon my way
With her silent spell.
Does she love me, Golden-rod?
Tell me, is all well?

21

A Pretty New Ballad, Entitled

Love And The Poet

In his bower the poet sat,
Caring not for this or that,
Troubled sore with love, and deeming
All but love but empty seeming.
How his heart did ache him! "Oh, it
Is too much!" quoth then the poet.

In his bower the poet lay,
Dreaming of his love all day.
When the stars came out at Night
No more joyed he at the sight.
Dreaming of his love. "I know it
Wears my life out," quoth the poet.

All the night and all the day
Dreamed the poet on alway.
Birds and flowers and hills and sea,
Sun and stars and moon and he
Lightly laughed no more. "Life, go! - - It
Brings no love," quoth then the poet.

Long he lay and long he muttered,
Knowing not what word he uttered;
Then he sprang him to his feet,
Burst in song and sang so sweet
Of his love, that birds flew to it,
"Hear my love-song," quoth the poet.

Long he sang and long they listened,
Tears within each bird-aye glistened,
"Sing thus to your love," they said,

"And, unless her heart be dead,
You will win her."
"I will do it,"
Quoth the simple, love-sick poet.

So he sang and so he won her;
Heaped his wealth of love upon her.
Lived and sang her praises out
To bird or man that came about.
Oh, what love! Their glad lives show it.
Happy maid and happy poet!

In his bower the poet sat,
Caring not for this or that.
Birds and flowers and rills and sea,
Sun and moon and stars and he
Lightly laughed once more.
"Ah, so it
Goes with love," quoth then the poet.

Kismet

At last, disheartened, in a quiet vale
I met a pure, unworldly, noble girl.
A woman then she grew, royally grand,
From each soft waving darkling curl
Kissing her thoughtful brow in shy content
Pressing her cheek in wanton merriment
From eyes all glorious, soulful, rare
From sweetest lips; from pearly cheeks; from blood
Mantling her snowy neck when I was there
Looked Love. I knew it then, and stood
Looking from Hell to Heaven and knew
That Heaven at last was mine - - Then grew

Her soul too great for earth; She died
And of that holy, perfect womanhood
Left was but this - - that I was satisfied
To know God's love and that His ways are good.

"Goodness finds strength where ???"

Palaces Of Air

For long these lovers lingered by the lake
And gave experience of their changing past - -
How he had loved her truly ere she knew
And guessed her heart was his, too, ere she knew
And laughed to see her pride ignore her love,
How love had come to him as sometimes cometh
The wanton spring from winter's long embrace
Leaping in perfect beauty ever great,
But she had fought against it, knowing not,
'Twere worse than useless fighting 'gainst herself.
And then they talked of other days when he
Had gone far from her, trusting in her faith
And knowing that her love was evermore,
While she had waited patiently at home
Till his return had crowned her happiness
And then of other little things that they
Had pleasure in the iteration of
And so on through the lengthened happy list
Anatomizing all their true love-life.

Slowly they stroll adown a tree-arched lane
Flower-sprent and beautiful and blossoming
In all the colors of the maiden Spring
Filling to Summer's womanhood.

24

At length
They pause to breathe the beauteous quietude--
The noblest pair of loving hearts, I think,
That e'er kissed lips or wandered down a lane,
And yet a shadow wreathed his brow and trouble
Looked from his eyes and from his downward glance
A tear stole softly. And as if toward
All dark thoughts from him in this happy hour
He caught his fair young sweetheart in his arms.
Her dark hair fell against his throbbing heart,
A silken skein for love to nestle in
And there abide forever. Silently
He pressed her to him, kissed her, then apart
Held her to gaze into her very soul
Till, with a fond start, she upward threw her arms
And clasped his neck, and nestled in his heart
And bade him rid himself of vain alarms
"Let love be ours" she said, "nor mind the rest."
Then grew he full of hope--

"Ay, Sweet," he said
"Our life shall be as this green, flowery lane,
All bright about and shaded overhead--
O my sweet love, was ever love like ours?"
The wedding day was set, " 'Twill be," they said,
"When Summer days and Summer flowers have fled
And Autumn's sheaves are gathering in the barns."
And many happy hours the lovers spent
Wandering and talking of the great to be
And building fancy palaces of air.

A Chapter Of Sorrow

I stood within our chamber late one night,
Our chamber, ours, my sweet, sad wife's and mine.
And, weary, gazed without in seeming sight,
Yet saw but tear-dimmed ghosts of "auld lang syne."

I saw two proud young lovers, lover-wise
Standing adown a flower-sprent, tree-arched lane,
Her young face on his shoulder in the guise
He loved so well; while in a silken skein.

Her dark hair fell against his throbbing heart.
--"Round her glad waist his arms he softly stole,
And pressed her to him, kissed her, then apart
Held her to gaze into her very soul.

Till with a fond start she upward threw her arms
To clasp his neck and nestle on his breast,
And bade him rid himself of vain alarms.
"Let love be ours," she said, "nor mind the rest."

Then he grew full of hope. "Ay, love," he said,
"Our life shall be as this green, flowery lane,
All bright about and shaded overhead.
O my sweet love, no twain such as we twain!"

II

Alas! for the long years that have been ours,
Alas! for the joys that soon came and went,
Alas! for the shading trees and blooming flowers,
Alas! for the hope that too soon was forspent.

III

Then, as I stood, lost, by the window-side,
My wife, my grief-pale wife, stole gently up,
Clad all in white with bare bosom that vied.
--Ah, God! but ours has been a bitter cup!--

As of old she put her soft arms around
My neck and nestled to my heart; but wept,
Wept oh! so hopelessly. 'Twas then I found
New heart to bid her calm, for hope but slept.

Yet still she sobbed; and her loose, flying hair
Streamed o'er us both, and wrapped us twain in one.
(The moon was hid neath clouds, but higher there
Appeared to be clear sky where cloud was none.)

"Look, love," I cried, "Be comforted, just as
Your moon sails through its present clouds, so we,
A little while and through them all we pass
To that undreamed-of future soon to be.

My sweet wife ceased her sobs and watched the moon,
While to the dark hair I my warm lips bowed.
But oh! dead hope! She piteously sobbed soon;
For what I thought clear sky was darker cloud.

Visions

There come to me sometimes
In faintest echo-rhymes
High messages of beauty all unknown,
It seems too rare and pure
For mortal to endure
The knowledge of the untempered truth alone.

27

For tho with mind intense
I strive to catch their sense
The music breaks and faints and dies away,
And sweet, with such regret
As angels feel "Not yet"
Breathes out as softly as the death of day.

But by those messages
My soul so lifted is,
That I, Columbus-like, no longer grope,
For these far-drifted signs
From Truth's remote confines
Assure me of the New World of my hope.

❧ ❧

The Angels Of Pity

In the way to the gate of the City,
Of the beautiful City of Light,
Wait the merciful angels of pity
For souls that may come in the night;
And they wait with their hands lightly folded,
With the tears yet unshed in their eyes,
Like the song in a poet-heart moulded
That never escaped in its sighs.

And they wait there forever and ever,
God's angels of mercy and love,
Tho they hear the glad roll of the river
That flows by the City above,
For they left all the light and the gladness
To free weary souls of their fears,
For they knew well this earth and its sadness,
And they could not be happy in tears.

In the day of the body's undoing,
When life shall have gone like a breath,
We shall lose the dread phantoms, pursuing
To the veriest verges of death;
For afar from the light of the City,
In the way to the portal thereof,
We shall meet the sweet angels of pity,
The inviolate angels of love.

A Thought

I caught tonight from out the vanished Past
A song I heard once only long ago;
Its subtle sweetness I had come to know
At last.

And so, I thought, the good we may have done
May lie unfelt within some heart for years,
Till that chance time the loving end it bears
Is won.

The Love-Tree

Love is a tree that just hath borne
Two flowers, one white and fair,
The other, dark and stained and torn
As dead Lucretia's hair.

The one breathes death; the other makes
The air all fresh and sweet
With life that throbs and faints and breaks
Like echoes in retreat.

A woman stands before the tree.
'Tis hers, the gift of one
Who held no dearer thing might be
Than it beneath the sun.

What flower her doubting hand shall save
Determines once for all
Love's future -- if it be a grave,
Or one long madrigal.

For if she pluck the dead, dark flower
Of Doubt, how love will grow!
But if she pluck fair Hope, that hour
The tree hath fallen low.

The Buried City

Centuries ago a city, fair and olden,
Stood by a sea that kissed its busy piers;
Loud clanged its bells, in mightly turrets holden,
Day in and out through all the changing years.

Great was its good and wide-spread was its glory,
True were its men, its women fair and pure;
Far o'er the earth was told its wondrous story,
And strangers came to see and make assurance sure.

Long stood it there, of all fair towns the fairest,
There walked God's angels, unseen sentinels,
There love was told -- O, story sweetest, rarest! --
Throbbing fond hopes in union with the bells.

Time came, alas! when Sin found out its portals,
And all the angels fled and goodness ceased to be,
Death came to claim the God-forsaken mortals,
The city fell and sunk beneath the friendly sea.

Long years have gone, yet still, when Earth is singing
"Glory to God" on holy, festal days,
Borne on the air men hear the old bells ringing
Far, faint and dim, their symphony of praise.

So to the heart grown old in doubt and sighing,
Buried deep down in man's self-centered thought,
Come there at times the echoes, faint and dying,
Of boyhood's trusting faith a loving mother taught.

No Title

There's his sister - that girl in deep black, Sir,
　　She thinks she's above me - how fool!
She's been always hard down on my back, Sir,
　　Since we both sat together at school.
An' I don't have much faith in her sorrow,
　　For there ain't much true sorrow in clo'e's,
　　　　But I - I'm only nobody,
　　But it's broken my heart, God knows.

His wife? So. I'm not his wife, Sir.
　　But I might ha' been that, by an' by.
An' I wouldn't give much for my life, Sir,
　　An' I'd like to just lay down an' die.
For I'm certain sometimes that I'm crazy,
　　An' I think that the craziness grows.
　　　　For I - I'm only nobody,
　　But its broken my heart, God knows.

31

Yes, he's dead. Bill's dead. Is God good, Sir?
Is he merciful, lovin' an' kind?
Then ask him - I can't - that he would, Sir
Take me too, for no one would mind.
An' I guess that his mother's hard hit, Sir,
An' his sister cares some, I suppose.
But I - I'm only nobody,
But it's broken my heart, God knows.

November 11, 1886
Room 98
W.D.H.

Only Nobody

Bills' dead, sir, dead. Is God good, sir?
He wasn't much more'n a boy.
But he died like a Christun man would, sir,
Kind o' filled with a holy-like joy.
An' I guess he's gone up to that Heaven
Where an angel like him only goes;-
- - But I - - I'm only nobody,
But it's broken my heart, God knows.

See that woman? - - that old woman there, sir;
That's his mother - - poor soul - - how she weeps!
Her face is as white as her hair, sir,
An' she moans like a babe when she sleeps.
She won't last long, either. That's certain.
She'll go with the winter's first snows.
- - But I - - I'm only nobody,
But it's broken my heart, God knows.

She hates me. I bear no ill will, sir.
I can't love or hate anymore.
But she tried to do all to get Bill, sir,
Not to meet me down there by the shore.
- An' I guess she was right. - An' I'm sorry,
Now he's dead an' her cup overflows;-
For I - - I'm only nobody - -
- But it's broken my heart, God knows.

There's his sister - - that girl in deep black, sir,
She thinks she's above me - - poor fool!
She's been always hard down on my track, sir,
Since we both sat together at school.
- An' I don't have much faith in her sorrow,
For there ain't much true sorrow in clo'e's;-
- But I - - I'm only nobody,
But it's broken my heart, God knows.

His wife? No. I'm not his wife, sir;
But I might ha' been that, by an' by;
An' I wouldn't give much for my life, sir,
An' I'd like to just lay down an' die;
For I'm certain sometimes that I'm crazy,
An' I think that the craziness grows,
For I - - I'm only nobody,
But it's broken my heart, God knows.

Yes he's dead - Bill's dead. Is God good, sir?
Is he merciful, lovin' an' kind?
Then ask Him - - I can't - - that He would, sir,
Take me, too, for no one 'ould mind;
An' I guess that his mother's hard hit, sir,
An' his sister cares some, I suppose;
- But I - - I'm only nobody,
But it's broken my heart, God knows.

November 11, 1886
Room 98
W.D.H.

33

The Scene Of The Tale

Long, level vistas of dim-reaching green,
Enframed on either side with giant hills,
Shade afar off where murky distance fills
The darkened daylight with its muffled mien.

The steady, weary down-pour of the rain
Falters, while scudding clouds drive o'er: then stops.
Comes a soft after-lude of falling drops,
While breaks of hum of voices o'er the plain.

A cock crows proudly and a sweet voice sings;
A bare-foot child freaks in the freedom given;
And lo! high o'er the sullen arch of Heaven,
Spanning the plain, a Bow of Promise springs.

The Scene Of The Telling

Indoors a laughing party meets--
A happy-hearted throng;
And as each merry youngster greets
"Dear Uncle Jack" each voice entreats
A story or a song.

With kindly look he sees their joy
And smiles, as he re-calls
Old days when he, a bright-haired boy,
With fairy, prince and maiden coy,
Dwelt in enchanted halls.

Each fresh young face with pleasure wells,
Each eager eye invites;
Then silent, as by magic spells,
They hear the pretty tale he tells
Of Iris and her sprites.

I

Once on a time - - a time long, long ago
Which means, my dear, the date I do not know,

There lived upon a rainbow high in air
A fairy queen named Iris fine and fair;

And with her lived and did the things she told them
And hardly ever gave her cause to scold them

Her little sprites - - a merry, busy lot
Who never said "I can't" or "I forgot."

And there they lived as happy as you please
And busy as the busiest of bees.

One day Queen Iris, dressed in colors bright,
Was smiling at each merry little sprite

Who sped along the lines of various hue
To keep them bright for her light sandal-shoe.

She was the sweetest, loveliest rainbow queen
That any sprite in all his life had seen.

And when she travelled, on good deeds intent
A rainbow formed the path she always went.

Her hair was shining like the bright sun-light
Her eyes were deep sky-blue, her skin milk white.

And round her flowing hair and in it twined
She wore a crown of six bright points combined.

Each point was all one color and one sprite
Was clad in that same color day and night;

And all he had to do was to keep clean
That single color for the rain-bow queen.

35

All were held equal and when Iris strayed
They played more pranks than you have ever played.

Today they worked away, now swift, now slow,
They polished up the colors of the Bow;

Still worked they gaily on, now up, now down,
And polished, too, the colors of her crown.

And all went merry and Queen Iris smiled
To see her sprites so happily beguiled.

II

But soon a growing murmur filled the air,
And dim the colors grew for lack of care,

While boastful sprites in hot dispute were seen
And discord reigned where harmony had been.

Now one spoke vauntingly and then another,
Each thought that he was better than his brother,

And soon they all forgot both heaven and earth
In boasting of their own peculiar worth.

One sprite who wore a garb of burning red
Grew redder still and to the others said:

"I am the worthiest. You all are good,
But could not be what I am if you would.

I am the color of the blood that flows
Within the veins of all our friends and foes.

What greater worth than mine?"

Then up spoke one,
(Who waited till the other sprite had done)

"Ha, ha!", he laughed: "And, pray, Sir, who are you
That dares compare himself with me, the blue?

My color fills all heavens highest space,
Not one of you can boast a higher place,

And down on earth none more than I can be,
Because I fill the ocean, lake and sea.

"No, no, I am the worthiest."

Then spoke
A laughing sprite who thought it all joke:

"Well, well," he said, "it's plainly to be seen
You haven't either one considered green.

You see me on the grass, the flowers, the trees.
I think the palm is mine, Sirs, if you please."

Then laughed the pompous purple sprite. "Ah, yes
I see you don't discern my worthiness.

I am the royal purple. I attend
All Kings and princes who to no one bend,

So I am worthiest."

The other two
Spoke of their worth, and loud the quarrel grew.

Then spoke they all at once, and soon
Their clatter
Called forth Queen Iris to decide the matter.

III

She came in all her splendor, while her eyes
Glanced round about her in a mute surprise.

Her crown of colors brightly gleamed and flashed - -
Each sprite bowed humbly and sank down abashed.

Then asked she what was wrong and when she knew
A smile crept softly forth to meet their view.

"O foolish sprites," she said, "to waste a minute
In such contention when there's nothing in it.

Now know you this, and know it once for all,
So that you ne'er again in error fall,

That all are equal and that none is better,
Nor to his fellow-sprites at all a debtor.

Let me not hear another word in wrath,
Or I at once dismiss you from my path.

And ere I now you to your work dismiss
Behold! the proof I give you is but this."

She took her crown whereon each color gleamed
And twirled it as before her sprites she beamed,

And lo! each color vanished from their sight
And there was but one ring of dazzling white.

The End

III

Weep, goddess, weep!
Till surcease of thy worn-eyed sorrow come.
Tear thy hair, beat thy breast, bid love be dumb,
And soft-souled sleep
Forsaken know not!

Curse the gods and die!
Or living, be a slave and bow thou down.

38

Put off thy goddess-hood and doff thy crown,
Thy pride put by
and let joy show not!

Aye, bruit thy grief!
Let flash of eye and quiver of lid and heave
Of fragrant bosom love no more deceive.
Be love's relief
Now in thy fate.

Thy pride has been,
Put off thy golden girdle of glad light,
And in coarse cloth of common earth-dark dight,
Muffle thy mien,
Misfortunate!

IV

Surcease of pain, O Queen, when this hard hurt,
By deadening depths of time lethean girt,
Shall heal, will bring thee back thy peace again,
No more thy lips curse God, thy salt tears spurt;
When thou shalt have at last for this cursed bane
Surcease of pain.

But I, who love her so that ev'n to die
Would bring no rest, or ease me of the cry
My anguished heart moans forth in sad refrain - -
What power in heaven or hell shall bid it fly
Now that she loves me not? When shall I gain
Surcease of pain?

The sad sea groans remonstrant to the earth;
The wild wind brings a woeful wail to birth;
The dark grave yawns and tells me hope is slain.
Without her love what are the ages worth?
Woe! woe! woe! I ask, but ask in vain
Surcease of pain.

An Offering To Love

Shy, blushing Morn light-kissed the winking strand,
  A thousand voices welcomed 'down the lake.
  Athwart the sky fled fast a shadowy band,
  That, soft-pressed by her rose be-dowered hand,
  Yet paused or dallied not even for her sake.

Then walked she, chaste, through forests silver-tongued,
  That sang her praise 'mid incense passing dear;
  Then, 'mid a swelling angelus, prolonged
  By nacreous naiads that around her thronged,
  She bathed her beauties in the clasping mere.

But when she to my dear love's chamber came,
  And first saw her so perfect, lying there,
  She burned more rosy with an envious flame
  At sight of beauty putting hers to shame,
  And smote her, coward-like and in despair.

Then grew her face cloud-dark, and from her eyes
  Poured waster of bitter tears, and down her cheeks
  --Her cheeks erst rapid-flushing red where sighs
  Of godly lovers brake in passionate guise,
  Changed soon to baffled rage and love-mad shrieks--

Ran tears, and through her close-pressed hands ran tears,
  And from her flaunting hair, and down her neck,
  And 'tween the orbid peaks her breast uprears,
  Down to her pink feet, in a flood that sears,
  Ran bitter tears born of her great pride's wreck.

That day that damned so wondrous, gleeful, glad,
  And 'nounced, preluding, while the soft sounds drove,
  Music, gold winged, turned woeful, wailing sad
  And wreaked in discords that all hope forbade
  Harsh teen of Morn's eclipse by my rare love.

40

II

My love awoke in wonder, unaware
What envious hand had caused her wakening,
And waking, blushed, and blushing, 'gan to sing,
Trilling a love-song set to merry air.
The samite beauty of her curling hair
Her eyes, her lips, her bosom quivering,
Were like - - were like? - - were unlike anything
And speechless spake nor did her heart forswear.

O sweet my love, come to thy window, pray,
And grant return for thy poor lover's sighs;
Assure him of a perfect, holier day
Than any his faint heart can now devise;
O come to me, and come, too, love, to stay,
And love me, love, and know no more disguise.

Haunted

Pressing her hands, I look into her eyes,
Her deep, sad eyes, filled with a wan despair,
That look not off or hold me in surprise. -- --
Is she meek sister sorrow sitting there,
Sorrow that comes and stays, and never dies?
Like a soft shroud floats out her ashen hair
And seems to wind me with her in its strands,
Pressing her hands.

Sees she the meeking shapes of loves that died, - -
Men's loves, passionate, strong, killed of false hope,
Maiden's loves, strangled at birth by false pride,
Midst ruins of broken hearts where they grope?
Sees she my love in its bier by her side,
My poor, trusting love, with great wounds that ope?
O! I bury my head where her breast expands,
Pressing her hands.

41

Perplexity

Are her eyes dark or light?
I never can tell.
I wondered last night
Are her eyes dark or light?
They are witchingly bright,
And potent their spell.
<u>Are</u> her eyes dark or light?
I never can tell.

War

Scene -- A quiet street of a quiet village. A little lad and a
littler maid. To these, the poet.

The little maid addresseth the poet.	I am just three years old. Mama told me I must never trust Billy Bold,
Pointeth to the lad and telleth of his wickedness.	Else, be rolled in the dust.
Requesteth a favor.	Please, won't you get me this great big stick?
Promiseth a reward.	If you do, You may kiss--
The mischievous lad maketh a suspicious move.	Hit him, quick!

The Songs That Were Sung Of Old

The songs that were sung of old!
Were they not whispers of fate?
Mingling a tear with a joy untold,
A dirge-like wind through a merry wold,
That strain that shall never abate.

The songs that were sung of old!
How they come back to me now!
Soft, clear and sad is their measureless plea,
Like sea-shells that echo a sound of the sea,
How shall I answer them, how?

The songs that were sung of old!
Can we not sing them again?
Heads have grown weary and hearts have grown cold,
Bells rung at marriage at death have been tolled,
Telling the story of men.

The songs that were sung of old!
No, ne'er again to be sung.
Only a perfume, faint, uncontrolled,
Floats from that mystical flower of gold
That bloomed in the days we were young.

Two Poems

A poet-child dreams by the orchard-gate,
With a poem of Love and a poem of Hate.

The smile that brightens the bonny face
Flees on the instant and leaves not a trace,
While the baby-hand clenches in ireful grace.

Blossoms and leaves frame the picture for me,
Wonderful picture for mother to see!

The poem of Love is the sweet, glad smile that died;
The poem of Hate, the little clenched fist by his side.

My Love

The sun-low-sinking- says farewell.
The ancient rose-bush sheds a flower.
The clear tones of a silver bell
Chime out the lovers' trysting-hour;
But to no love-illumined bower
My damsel her lover calls:
Caught up by some far, magic power,
I muse in olden, golden halls.

My love is far away, but I
In thought draw all her spirit near
Her simple days are passing by
In thought of me -- so dear! so dear!
But do I more to her appear
Than she to me is? -- Nay, not so!
She is so much my life, I hear
Her heart-throbs and their meaning know.

44

No wondrous king of kingly man
More honored was than now am I.
No victory won of Saracen
E'er gained a knight reward as high;
For tho no cringing courtiers fly
To win my lady's smiled compense,
No queen's false majesty can vie
With her sweet, truth-crowned innocence.

And she is beautiful! Her face
So pale so pure, so pearly fair,
That when she blushes I can trace
A subtle, unknown splendor there!
The glowing of her flowing hair
Is like the lustrous dark of night.
Her perfect lips are seals to care;
Her eyes a sea-green depth of light.

And yet I think not of my love
As other than so nobly good,
Not any power below, above,
Could soil her loyal womanhood.
She is God's noblest work. O would
The earth hold many such as she,
That from their love and faith man should
Gain strength to true nobility.

1885

A Bibliophile

"The bibliophile -- The true lover of books -- is
he who buys to read and to enjoy" -- G. A. Sala.

You read of "book-men" nowadays,
Since men have taken on this craze
Of "book-collecting";

45

And steady students now no more
Are "book-men" in the sense of yore. - - -
　　　'Tis most affecting.

I'm one who has a few old books,
And loves the quiet, winning looks
　　　Of peace about them.
I cannot tell, even with their aid,
What I, by fortune's hand betrayed,
　　　Should do without them.

Some are old friends of many years.
Some have been witnesses of tears;
　　　And all, of sparkle.
Some have been bought and read but once;
Some read so oft their worn old fronts
　　　Are patriarchal.

Most of them are a modest lot,
A student's loved "without which not,"
　　　And no "collection."
All are my friends and all are good,
Whether I read in merry mood,
　　　Or deep dejection.

There are not many richly dight,
And few that shine in borrowed right
　　　Of age or rareness.
Do Caxton, Aldine, Elzevir,
Giunta, Petit, et cet. confer
　　　More worth in fairness?

But let "collectors" still "collect."
To these now "book-men" all respect;
　　　I'm out of fashion.
I'll buy "to read and to enjoy." - -
A habit formed when still a boy
　　　Has grown a passion.

To A More-Than-Friend

Amidst a jarring horror of discord
A flute-note fell, sweet as a summer's bird,
Revealing Heaven to the heart that heard;

Above a vale of barrenness and woe,
Where rugged desolation only was,
A bird sang, carolling of hope and love;

Up through the darkness of a muddy lake
A clear, pure spring threw waters glistening,
That diamonded the darkness for an hour;

Athwart the drear November of a life
A violet-spangled May-day came and went;
And from that day it knew the flush of joy;

So unto me you came, Poor payment I
Can ever make in our heart-reckoning.
--A beetle giving tribute to a rose.

So, when I knew you first. But, ah! you stayed
And gained me mastery o'er weakling self.
I give you reverence as of slave set free.

The Mate Of The Imogen

Recited January 7, 1885, -- Pennsylvania College

'Twas morn when we sailed from the silent port,
'Twas morn of a glorious day,
But the mates' eyes fell as we passed the fort,
And they laughed not once with their wonted sport,
As we swiftly sailed away.

For the church-yard held in a grassy plot
His sweet young wife at rest;

47

And his heart was there in that sacred spot
With the birds as they sang "forget me not"
To the flowers above her breast.

His joy was full and his heart was glad
When we sailed from port before;
And the vessel danced on like a ship gone mad,
And the winds howled loud and long and sad--
But the mate laughed all the more.

But now what change! For his eyes glared round
In a way to tear one's heart,
And they looked so strange at the slightest sound,
That his men kept back as he stared and frowned,
And sadly stood apart.

He was thinking how she, as he held her hand,
When the end of her life drew near,
Had said, "If ever, when lost to land,
You feel in need of a helping hand,
Remember that I am near."

And little he knew as the whisper fell
On that hushed, hallowed air,
How soon the echo of love's farewell
Would greet his soul as a dying knell,--
But that was all his prayer.

For so it was. On that very night,
The good ship Imogen,
Sailing away like a bird of flight,
Was met by a squall of fearful might,
And doomed seemed all her men.

Now high on the crest of a wave she soared,
Then down in the trough she fell;
And the mighty winds around her roared;
And the waves through every opening poured,
And the horror none can tell.

The night wore on, and all seemed lost,
When lo! The moon burst through,
And there by its silvered rylots crossed
At the helm with her golden hair out-tossed,
The mate's wife faced the crew.

Up sprang the mate of the Imogen,
And turned with a face alight,
And cried to the crew "Have courage, men,
We'll save her yet, please God;" and then
He turned him to the night.

And lo! the clouds were scattering far,
And the wind's wild rush was stayed;
And there in the distance gleamed a star,
While the moonlight glimmered on rope and spar
As they hither and thither swayed.

Then a wild cry rose through the startled night,
For the mate in the tossing green
Had fallen, and yet with a calm delight
On his face, sank slowly out of sight,
And never more was seen.

That's the end of the tale. When the sun appeared
On the morrow, clear and bright,
The ship, though crippled, was safely cleared,
And the helmsman took her and home he steered,--
But none forgot that night.

And what of the mate's wife, did you say?
Nothing, that I can tell.
From the time that the mate fell to this day
Some doubt the occurrence; some only say
She vanished when all was well.

Jim: A "Round Unvarnished Tale"

Jim was an ugly, cross-eyed lad,
Who lived in the heart of the mountain.
But little of joy in life he had,
And that, he said, "not wuth countin'."

His home was up where the pine trees grew,
Far off from the sight of man;
And Jim had nothing on earth to do,
But to roam all day, and then

Come back to his wretched home at night
To be scolded and cuffed by his mother,
And when his father was out of sight
To be sworn at and kicked by his brother.

So as Jim grew up he soon began
To vanish for days together,
And plotted when he became a man,
He'd cut from this slavish tether.

He'd kill his brother and run away,
And if any one followed after,
He'd kill him too. - - It seemed so gay
That he nearly choked with laughter.

II

Only birds and trees were friends to Jim,
And he told them all his woe;
The trees tried to make amends to him
And the birds sang soft and low.

Still his heart was sad and his life was mean,
And his face was set in a frown,
Till when his years counted up thirteen,
His parents moved into the town.

III

"Ah, now," thought Jim, "I shall now begin
    To live as a boy should live."
But his deepest troubles had just come in,
    And the town no joy could give.

For Jim had never yet been to school,
    And knew not his a-b-c's,
And the other boys called him a fool,
    And the girls did nought but tease.

So a year dragged on and no hope came.
He was shunned by both high and low,
And Jim's fierce spirit began to tame,
    And his wounded heart to show.
Unhappy at school, unhappy at home,
    Unhappy wherever he went.
His never-strong mind was overcome
When his last faint hope was spent.

IV

So one day Jim, with his father's gun,
    As the sun sank in the West,
Concluding his short life-work was done,
    Shot himself dead. Let him rest.

Then the town-folk shuddered and talked and sighed
    "That miserable boy!" they said,
While Jim - - poor Jim - - as for that he died,
    Was happy, I hope, with the dead.

His story is brief and rudely writ,
    And simple. There are more of his kind.
But to any who reads and thinks on it
    A moral therein he may find.

In The "Old Dominion"

Daisy of the dark-blue eyes,
Saucy, pretty Daisy,
Wandered with the dashing Hal
In the meadows hazy.
Cupid watched them from afar,
High on hopeful pinion.
--This occurred some years ago
In the "Old Dominion."

Daisy was a charming girl,
Hal, her sworn defender;
Daisy had sweet wilful ways,
Hal grew very tender.
Cupid drew a little near
On more hopeful pinion.
--This occurred some years ago
In the "Old Dominion."

Walks grew frequenter and far.
Heart for heart was given.
Daisy was the only star
Shining in Hal's heaven.
Cupid knew the game was his,
For, in his opinion,
Gallant Hal was now a slave
In the old dominion.

Yesterday

I sing of buds that shrink and die
Before they bloom upon the way
Where dim and gray the shadow lie
Of vanished Yesterday.

I had an idol called a friend;
It proved to be of basest clay.
I loved: My love should have no end.
- - - - Alas! 'Twas yesterday.

All plans are vain. All life is filled
With Expectation's sure decay,
And hopes are born but to be killed
And laid with Yesterday.

They gleamed like pebbles on the shore
Made beauteous by the dashing spray,
Till o'er them rolled forevermore
The waves of Yesterday.

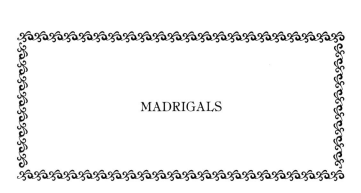

MADRIGALS

Sing To Me, Love

Sing to me, love,
The song you sang at evening long ago;
And I shall think that Luna youth has come
To sway again, with restless ebb and flow,
The tide of vernal passion long grown dumb.
Sing to me, love.

Sing to me, love.
Your gentle voice grows sweeter with the years,
And all old songs, for loving hearts, are best.
Sing sweet, sing soft, sing low, -- for night appears,
And signs are stealing from his deep, calm breast.
Sing to me, love.

Sing to me, love,
And let the old song bear our spirits up
To greet each happy star and bid it shine.
The tears of life fall thick in every cup,
But love exalts them into smiling wine.
Sing to me, love.

Sing to me, love.
Sing sweet the old, old song, -- sing sweet and low,
And kiss me when the fain refrain is done;
And I shall know, though passion come and go,
That love is warm and constant as the sun.
Sing to me, love.

Margaret

'Tis peaceful now:
A holy glad sereneness fills the earth
And yet, I know not why nor how
Myriads of fairy voices falling, falling
From the great otherwhere, give joyous birth
To music so divine, so sweet, so thrilling
I faint to hear these glorious voices filling
The air with one grand madrigal of Love!
I wake, and, lo! they're calling, calling, calling
From far ethereal balconies above
The name of one whose gentle, tender presence
Hovering forever near me in the busy mart
Of worldly selfishness, doth bid all else depart
Save Love and Hope and Peace. E'en dull Care lessons
And Misery smiles at sight of her sweet face - -
Ah! They're already going. Fainter and fainter still - -
As if they go swayed by some stronger will
And much against their own, - - the airy space
Echoes their tremulous bliss. And now they're gone!

They're gone. And yet, and yet,
Earth, air, trees, rocks, glens, rivers, dales,
All Nature's volumes of all nature's tales
Echo the story of the days we met
And ring into my dazed ears the sound
Of one dear name, pure as its emblem found
In deep blue depths of ocean. Where'er I go,
They breathe it lovingly, they breathe it low,
The name, sweetest of all names as yet,
The name of - - Margaret.

August 3, 1884

Margaret
Photo Courtesy of the Brenner Family

At Evening

Flowers are exhaling their day-misered sweets,
Star-sets are gemming the sea;
Fond eyes are watching the day-bloom that fleets,
But I watch thee.

Softly the sweet serenades are up-lift,
Softly sway sapling and tree;
Wavelets are kissing fair blossoms that drift,
But I kiss thee.

One more sweet day of our life gone, my own,
Sweet, love, for me and for thee.
Night soon grown cool, lacking love that has flown,
But never we.

Marguerite
A Love-Song

If in my dreams I see
One tender face,
Can you not pardon me,
Knowing her witchery,
You in my place?
No dream could be complete
Lacking my Marguerite.

When I arise I hear
Always one name.
If birds love her and cheer
Me by their praise of her,
Are they to blame?
So they trill love and sweet,
Marguerite, Marguerite.

Sweet as a late-blown rose,
Cheers she my way;
Freely her sweetness goes,
Royally forth it flows,
Sweeter each day.
Good doth itself repeat
Daily with Marguerite.

Wind, to thy gentle care
These lines I trust.
Bear them hence anywhere;
Tell all you meet of her;
Tell them you must.
Do not, I beg, secrete
My song of Marguerite.

Face To Face

Proudly she turns -- as palely fair as pearl,
And holy as the Blessed Damosel;
Reluctant lips seem opening to tell
Some sweet sincerity or subtle spell
That varies with the heart-beats of a girl.

II

Her eyes are riddles for my heart to read;
Now brimmed with joy, now dark and sad as pain;
Now clear as heaven, deep-souled, and fresh as rain;
Now non-committal as my love is plain,
And shy as placid when my own eyes plead.

III

The happy ribbon, flutt'ring at her throat,
Is not more spotless than her heart is pure, --
Sweet heart of hearts that beats so soft and sure
To time her words, half-reckless, half-demure,
-- And old-time music as of lute or rote.

IV

Her thoughts are wisdom born of innocence;
(A woman-girl she thinks girl-womanly.)
Her ways are winning as a girl's can be,
Yet softening into coy maturity.
--Her heart is mine when but her will consents.

The following poem is unsurpassed and unsurpassable (???....)

In fabled image rich and rare
And painting old and glorious
Portrayed in style beyond compare
By master hands victorious
Fair maidens clad in silk attire
With grand and noble bearing
Came forth with Love's inspiring fire
From eyes half-veiled but daring!
And humble virgins fair and sweet
In Love's fell web entangled
Look out in innocence complete
With flow'ry wreathes bespangled,
But artist's loves howe'er they be
In face or form bewitching
Can never, dearest, vie with thee
Or be to me so enriching
In love and joy. What <u>thou dost will</u>
Of happiness is mine, pet,
Thou art my sweet, my all, my fill
Of gladness and regret,
And may I be forever still
If thee I e'er forget.

My Margaret

Last night I met a haughty set
Of ladies stiff and grand
They seemed to me indeed to be
The proudest in the land.
And they were dressed in very best
And they were fair to see
But Margaret, my Margaret
Is fairer far to me.

The bird that sings on out-stretched wings
The gladness of his nest
He little cares what envy shares
Possession of my breast.
The wind that blows by every rose
Is wailing through the tree
That Margaret, my Margaret
Is far away from me.

I watch the gray old shadows play
Along the ivied walls
I watch them chase across their face
At certain intervals.
But still the thought will not be fought
Of home across the sea
Where Margaret, my Margaret
Is waiting now for me.

Dear little wife -- God grant my life
Be spent with thee at home
When once again the watery main
Is crossed -- no more to roam.
Let others shun the trust that's won
I want my home and thee!
For Margaret, my Margaret
Is more than all to me.

A Secret

Hide it deep in the depths of your roses, cherie,
  Blushing roses confusion discloses, cherie,
    Let it sleep in their keep till it die
    Like a star in the sun-lighted sky,
  Out of sight in the infinite closes, cherie,
    Of the heaven the poets espy.

But to me it is open forever, cherie,
  Spite of pride and its wildest endeavor, cherie,
    Though I chance but to glance at your face
    All its share of our care I can trace,
  Yet I fear not for years, maybe never, cherie,
    Shall we come to ourselves and embrace.

Let us dream of a brighter tomorrow, cherie,
  A tomorrow unladen of sorrow, cherie,
    When the day will repay all our pain,
    And the night will delight us again,
  While the Past will but vanish afar, O, cherie,
    Like a storm that has chastened a plain.

Madge

Madge, with love in her eyes
Madge, with her soft replies
Madge, with her sweet heart beating steadily, surely true,
Let us go forth alone
You, love, you and I
Far from the hearts of stone
Far from the mean world's cry
Far -- to Love's green-pillared castle enarched with blue.

Soft under foot is the grass
Soft, where the swallows pass,
Is the billowy fold of tender sky that we love
Softer far is her hair
And her cheek by breezes fanned - -
Deeper, ah, deeper the bare
Warm clasp of her slender hand
Than the exceeding depth of the old, old sky above.

Warm, red lips and sweet
Kissed, me supine at her feet,
Kissed me a kiss that shall thrill my whole being for aye
Ah, cold moon, I am right - -
Hide your tear-pallid face
You may be Queen of Night,
But this girl, this pride of the race
This love-laden darling of mine, is the queen of the Day,

And queen of my heart, love-crowned,
Bringer of lost hope found
And sweetness of life to a rare intoxicant draught
Kiss me once more, my sweet
Once more loving and long
Repeat, repeat, repeat
Till the burden of song
Makes quiver the liquid in every fair rose-goblet quaffed.

The Touch Of Her Hands

She held me her hands, "It is over," I thought,
And the blossom of love falls a thorn at my feet.
Is it well that her hand - - the fair hand that I sought - -
Scatter hope's dying brands?
- - But, O, heart! what is this, so o'er powering, so sweet,
In the touch of her hands?

65

It is love, it is life, it is infinite bliss,
It is more than the veriest dreamer e'er dreams;
And there seems something more in the depth of her kiss
Than a man understands.
O! the soul of my darling reveals her and gleams
In the touch of her hands.

"God guard you," she said, and the light in her eyes
Thrilled love to the depths of a weary man's heart;
And the roseate flushes that waved in the skies,
Over seas, over lands,
Resembled high feelings that quicken and start
At the touch of her hands.

O, the touch of her hands is a wonder of love,
More tender than vision of days that are done,
And deeper than knowledge of angels above.
Too much! ah, too much!
Her heart and my heart are forever as one
Since the light of that touch.

My Marguerite

O Marguerite, my Marguerite,
A thousand blessings on thee, Sweet.
Thy life's a book of love, complete.

Gentle and proud and tender-wise
Time never walks near you. He flies
Catching the sunlight from your eyes--

Time never walks. He flies to tell
The good you do. He knows full well
How many hearts your praises swell.

How many a poor care-weary one
Cheered by thy whispered "nobly done"!
Bears up and on--a victory won!

These humble blessings always met
These mother's cheeks with glad tears wet
    Are jewels for God's coronet.

Oh! noble graceful Marguerite
My praise is nought to those that meet
    Your daily kindness-carrying feet.

All love thee and all give thee praise,
Pray God he let me end my days
    In happy influence of thy ways.

January 1885

Snow-Flake: A Fireside Fancy

Snow-flake! Snow-flake!
Help me for love's sake,
Fly to my sweet-heart and kiss her for me.
Fly to her,
Sigh to her,
Steal softly nigh to her,
Press her, caress her, possess her for me.

Snow-flake! Snow-flake!
Help my poor heart-ache,
Steal to my sweet-heart and kiss her for me.
Steal to her,
Kneel to her,
Gently appeal to her,
Press her, caress her, possess her for me.

Snow-flake! Snow-flake!
To my dear love take
Love's tender message and tell her for me.
Fall to her,

67

Call to her,
Give my heart's all to her,
Melt on her red lips and quell her for me.

Snow-flake! Snow-flake!
Help or my heart break;
Fly to my sweet-heart and kiss her for me.
Speak for me,
Seek for me
Do not be weak for me,
Press her, caress her, possess her for me.

Unfinished

O Margaret, my Margaret
The time is drawing near
It seems I've scarcely seen you, yet
Again must leave you, dear.
But loving hearts are faithful
And loving hearts are true
And the love that brings me to you
Will send me off anew.

There are not many things in life, I know,
That . . . . .

BALLADES AND RONDEAUS

A Ballade Of Life

When hearts and feet alike are light,
And youth, with Beauty, threads the maze,
When soft words make bright eyes more bright,
And Rose her first shy victim plays,
When poets write their maiden lays,
When vows are pledged in trembling wine,
When nights are only foils to days, --
May no unworthy place be mine.

When clouds begin to mar the sight,
And atra cura comes and stays,
When youth and beauty take to flight,
And rose-tints turn to sombre grays,
When Rose herself, with some amaze,
Finds in her hair a silver line,
When fire-light fancies no more blaze, --
May no unworthy place be mine.

Then, too, when winter's starlit night
Brings back to us our faded days,
When Rose's hair is snowy white,
And down the years her memory strays,
When Life is but an empty phrase,
And Love is something all divine, --
When all is won of blame or praise,
May no unworthy place be mine.

Envoy

When sun-light glints on glistening sprays.
When full-blown flowers fade and pine,
When, too, but ashes fill the vase,
May no unworthy place be mine.

71

Ballade Of An Objectionable Suitor

He is handsome and rich and all that,
And is quite universally "read."
He is never insipid or flat,
And knows when a thing is well-said.
His knowledge I really quite dread,
For, indeed, he's a creature apart;
I admire the fine shape of his head,
But he cannot appreciate "art."

He is master of racquet and bat,
And his dancing would quite turn your head;
He always knows what he is at
And has (for his size) a light tread.
They call him familiarly "Nod."
And, again, I assure you he's "smart";
But my strong admiration has fled--
For he cannot appreciate "art."

Our day on the bank as we sat,
By a whimsical humor misled,
We had a real practical chat
And he talked about "paupers" and "bread,"
Then he talked about love till I fled
And suggested we'd better depart.
He is sensible, witty, well-bred,
But--he cannot appreciate "art."

Envoy

Maidens! At last he has asked me to wed,
But I cannot believe in his heart,
And I'll take me his rival instead,
For he cannot appreciate "art."

72

Ballade Of Old Grave-Stones

Moss-grown and crumbling and old,
Stormed at by wind and by rain,
Yielding to heat and to cold,
Years adding stain into stain,
Rarely the lines still remain,
Writ in a quaint, simple rhyme,
Telling who conquered Life's pain. - - -
Lives are but servants of Time.

How many years have been doled,
Years spent for loss or for gain,
Since this pure, virginal mold
First had a date to sustain!
- - This was "created to Jane - - "
Hard to make out for the grime.
No other letters are plain. - -
Lives are but servants of Time.

Daisies bloom over the fold,
Caught in an intricate chain.
Sunlight is flocking with gold
Grave of devout and profane.
Down at the end of the lane
May-bells are ringing a chime.
Softly the stones yield refrain, - -
Lives are but servants of Time.

Envoy

Hark! A sweet bird's noble strain,
Perched on the stone 'neath the lime,
Bears the old burden again. - -
Lives are but servants of Time.

73

Ballade Of A Strong-Minded Girl

She is tall, intellectual, and bold,
And she seeks all her words to prolong,
She's about four-and-twenty years old,
And her mind is unusually strong;
She is "up" on each separate wrong
That "woman" is striving to wreak;
And she'll lecture a man or a throng,
But her heart is unusually weak.

Her voice is calm, distant and cold.
Great nonsense she thinks is a song.
Her projects she'll freely unfold,
For her mind is unusually strong.
She calls gentlemen "mes enfants,"
And ladies "so wretchedly meek,"
She indulges, sometimes, in Souchong,
And her heart is unusually weak.

She's acquainted with tongues manifold,
And alarms all the girls she's among;
She's a hearty despiser of gold,
For her mind is unusually strong.
When she walks she takes no one along,
But an old heathen Roman or Greek
And marriage, she says, is a thong,
For her heart is unusually weak.

Envoy

Prince, I feel my heart beat like a gong
But - - her mind is unusually strong;
Even then I'm half minded to speak,
But - - her heart is unusually weak.

74

Ballade Of A Scandal-Monger

I've <u>no</u> faults, (as everyone knows).
I aim to be open as day.
I always tell what "I suppose,"
And frankly explain what "they say."
My sympathy's always in sway
To ferret out everything "new,"
And I gossip at work and at play --
I'm one of the privileged few.

I know who are friends and who foes;
His debts I know one who won't pay;
I know all the belles and their beaus,
I know of a shocking affray;
I know a young man gone astray,
And unhappy marriages, too,
The secrets of all are my prey --
I'm one of the privileged few.

My knowledge I freely unclose.
My confidence you'll not betray?
Don't whisper a word unto those
Who are likely to "give it away."
(I tell the whole town in this way,
And the doings of all I review.)
I'm perfect myself, so I may --
I'm one of the privileged few.

Envoy

Friend, give ear to my warning, I pray.
Be careful of all that you do;
Or you'll find yourself served on a tray
By one of the privileged few.

75

To Mr. Isaac Walton

My line I cast full oft today,
And trod a weary, winding way;
Came back without a single trout,
Nor saw a milk-maid near about
Respect to whom I fain would pay.

Aye, but 'tis merry fun, I say,
Sometimes; but never, should there stray
An irate shout from brawny lout,
My line I cast.

Ik Walton, I would thou couldst play
My part, and be a helpless prey
To watch-dog stout with cruel snout
To wear your gentle spirit out. --
Still, take, this quiet eve of May,
My line I cast.

While Here I Lie

A rondeau to . . . .
(Who wonders how I spend my idle hours.)

While here I lie 'neath giant trees,
My fancy, wayward as the breeze,
    Drifts to an eve <u>we only</u> know.
    I live the old, sweet long-ago
Here in this flower-scented case.

Fair Memories all my spirit seize;
They bear me softly where they please.
    --I see you come, I see you go,
        While here I lie.

I see your sweet eyes sweeter grow
I see a new light in them glow.
I hold your hands. My doubting flees.
--What lowly-whispered words are these?
    I kiss your lips. "I love you so!"
        While here I lie.

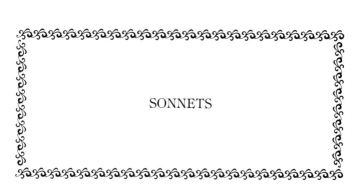

SONNETS

Could I But Do It

Could I but do it - - Could my heart and hand
But aid endeavor to sublime success - -
Could I but strike through all my native land
One ringing stroke for truth and nobleness
In song as martial as of drum and fife
Yet sweet and helpful as a dear one's tone
Then song were not in vain; and length of life
Might hold some beauty that were all its own.

Is it, O God, not right for me to pray
Knowing thy love embraceth every one
While yet I murmur, "Thy good will be done"
For strength to sing it ere I pass away?
Let me but one immortal chaplet twine - -
Thine be the glory and the service mine.

Reconciliation

When sweet my love in anger turned from me,
I blamed her in my injured heart and said
"She loved me not or else her love is dead,"
And cursed her cruel though none kind as she;
But when nepenthe came not sequently
And sore my heart was of such drearied,
I cursed my-self and doubt was buried - -
- - So sweet my love a-righted gan to be,
"For if," I thought, "my lady loved me not,
She had not so my constant heart misdeemed,
It is excess of love her spirits yilde";
Then prostrate at her feet her grace besought,
And back she to my tears her own beteemed - -
So sweet my love and I were reconciled.

A Reverie

To hear a music sweet as of a lyre,
To dream a dream of happiness to be,
To watch the swift mute shadows as they flee
Before the uncertain leapings of the fire;
To fancy sweet young faces - - Love's own choir - -
To see in this, her smiles; in that, maybe,
Her tears; in all impassionately to see
The yearning of her great proud love's desire.
To see a few years future melt away
Like sullen clouds before the all-conquering sun,
(How Love hates Time; Oh To trust, to hope, to pray
These days of weary waiting soon be done - -
This dull-droned prelude to that pregnant day
When Life is Heaven and Heaven's own bliss is won.

The Departure Of Sleep

At morn when night's sweet shadowy visions fade,
And voices of the day gin wanton chant,
And erst life's dolorous duties dimly haunt,
While dawns a sense of some lost love bewrayed,
They Sleep - - dear Sleep - - his lotted span out-stayed,
His soft wings hover in a gentle pant,
And brings he back my soul noctivagant,
And kisses he my eyes with tears embayed;
Then wanders as if shrinking from the light,
But lingers still, reluctant, within call,
Then comes again and makes soft, anguished moan;
Till when he starts and hastes in vain affright,
And on a swift sunbeam that smites the wall
He goes - - dear Sleep - - and leaves me wake and lone.

Love, Sleep And Death

When that mine eyes with dust of gold are sprent,
And Sleep, the rose-white son of Night, draws nigh,
It seems 'twere all of happiness to die,
If Death, his brother, brought such blandishment;
For then my soul is lapped in soft content,
And day-dreamed sweets no more my having fly,
And Love is all my own and I am I,
Knowing again the joys incontinent.

O Love, sweet Love, that comes now but in dreams!
O Sleep, sweet Sleep, that gives Love back to me!
How bare the sun-swept sand of day-life seems,
How green and full the shadowy mead with ye!
O Death, sweet Death! how vain my straggling themes,
If thou give this--fore'er with Love to be.

Sonnet

I've lived and loved. Death cannot change me this.
Though heaven and earth should pass away there still
Would be to me her love and her sweet will.
And memory of love's first, divinest kiss.
Love is enough--there is nought else we miss,
For craven Death may flaunt his power to kill
And Time--wise worldling--sigh and bode us ill,
But Love is Love and ours, and we are his.

Of all sweet truths 'tis sweetest in the earth,
And great above all greatness words imply,
And fraught of hopes that, taking sudden birth,
Like winged birds through all hereafter fly.
No more I dream! I know what Love is worth
--And Time and Death and Life and All defy.

83

To Sir Philip Sidney

O Sidney, poet-souled, let me not sing
With other words than simple, praising thee;
O constant heart, that loved so passionately
And burst in song in vain importuning;
O perfect life, whose flowery-crescent Spring
No Summer's fruit was destined e'er to see,
No flight of mine can wake fit eulogy,
For I, alas! fly but with broken wing.
But weeping once I found my damosel
A-sitting in a wood-pied field in June,
And listless by her side her white hands fell;
Then, as I pressed her close, the tell-tale moon
Shone on the page of love-smote Astrophel.
Could word of mine award thee higher boon?

In Memoriam
C. W. C.

As one who cometh oft with reverent tread
To pay his duty at a sacred shrine,
Where nobleness and wisdom did combine
To yield such other mastery of the dead; --
As one who saw a star flame overhead,
So liquid-pure its fire seemed like a wine,
That vanished as a vision superfine
And left him wondering memory instead; --
As one who saw a lily, floating pale
And beautiful upon the water's breast,
Engulfed forever by an angry flood; --
As one who saw a town, erect and hale,
Swept off by fell tornado of the West; --
So saw I Death's sad victory over Good.

Flora Bell Bikle

Died August 8, 1885

Such grace was hers we know she only came
To teach us all to love in her the good;
So sweet she grew to blessed maidenhood,
To us so much of all we loved, her name
The sadness of the saddest hearts o'ercame
And woke such smiles, such prayers none other could
Till that before the mystic door she stood
That opes from maiden's hope to woman's aim.

Then grew her soul too great for earth; she died;
And as we threw our flowers into her grave
It seemed they bloomed afresh in very pride
Of sacrifice to one more sweet than they: --
And we, dear God, have learnt thy lesson, save
We see not why our little lives may stay.

Unrevealed

As I sit
In my room,
Through the gloom
Shadows flit.
(What is it,
--That perfume?)
How they loom
To my wit!
But, alas!
I cannot
Catch their sense;
And they pass
From the spot
And go--whence?

85

My Lady's Cheek

I gave my love a last, a long farewell
And bore with me a bunch of faded flowers
That languished on her breast a few short hours
And died in envy of that lilied swell.
But why she gave them I could never tell
And wondered oft and wondering toned my powers
Till desperate I broke what stress was ours
To have her own sweet lips my doubt dispel - -
In vain the quest! Alas, she know not why
Or, knowing, could not for her blushes, speak
And yet no better answer needed I
For love is strong and words were ever weak
And then the flowers could do nought else but die,
My love re-blossomed with my lady's cheek.

Gettysburg, 1885

Along the shaded street a soft sound floats,
The quiet town's uninterrupted hum;
From fragrant fields balsamic odors come
Of wild-wood flowers and ripening wheat and oats.
The fading sun-light lingeringly gloats
On orchard-wall and bough of peach and plum. - -
No more the crack of arms or roll of drum
Or shriek of death or call of bugle-notes!
On Round Top's height the trees are fresh and green.
The light wind peers where hissing bullets drove,
Upon the grass-grown breast-works lightly lean
Two lovers whispering of a happy love,
While 'neath the sod, inviolably clean,
The dead have peace more full than that above.

Gettysburg Square - circa 1880
Photo Courtesy of the York County Historical Society

SWAN SONG

Dated Sonnets - Unfinished

November 19, 1886 – December 21, 1886

Swan Song

Her beauty passes all my youthful dreams
So fair she is, so firm and sweet of form,
I think her bosom is more white and warm
Than spring is happy or than in the beams
Of summer suns a summer ripeness streams.
Her eyes hold beauty as the coming storm
Holds rain, filled o'er-full with a siren swarm
Of shy desires that dance along their gleams.
Her words are sweet as Hygia's honey-pure
As Aeolian whispers -- intense as wine
That ripened on the fair companion shore.
She is to me as the bright stars that shine
In heaven -- She is so fair, yet so demure,
And unresponsive when I call her mine.

November 19, 1886

II

There have been times I've doubted if she cared
To hear me praise her beauty to her face,
As if all praise were scant or out of place
To one who knew the royal power she shared
With her for whom the father-poet dared
The shades of Pluto, that a woman's grace,
A kiss, a tear, a smile, a long embrace,
Is greatest dreamed of, longed for. Yet she bared
Her round, white arm to me one day and said
"What is it worth?" And I stood still as death
And whispered while my blood surged like a flood
"Heaven," and she smiled, half-pleased, and turned her head
Like Galatea drawing her first breath,
Wondring to see Pygmalion's passion bud.

November 20, 1886

91

III

Her eyes are like twin oceans in whose keep,
    Deep down in sapphire depths I seem to see
        The outline of a golden fair citie,
    Encircled with four mighty streams, with deep
        Flower-spangled sides; where virgins reap
        Great garlands of the fairest bloom to lay
        Before the naked feet of her whom they
Have crowned their queen. And lo! from all the heap
    She takes not one; but from her bosom where
        There rise and fall the roses of young love
    While, yet blushing, --purity, yet desire--
    She takes and makes a crown for me to wear
        For I'm to be her king, and she to prove
        The queen of virtue is a heart on fire.

November 20, 1886

IV

Ah! vain illusion! for the town I scanned,
    Spread out in beauty like a summer's night,
        Was not a vision that I saw aright,
    But one that in my dreaming soul I planned,
        And had so longed to see its like expand
        On hers that it was gleaming in my sight,
Transfixed within her luminous eyes whose bright
        Depth mirrored my fancied lover's land;
    I had but looked and dreamed I saw, made wild
    By something that I did see, struggling there
        To free itself and come and be my own.
    I think she loves me, though the wilful child
        That still lives in the woman will declare
        A love long-given, yet a love unknown.

V

I used to think to dream of her were all
I wanted - - just to drink her beauty in
As earth drinks light and heat - - a joy a-kin
To Adam's in the days before the fall,
When first he looked on Eve within the wall
Of Eden, and had never yet known sin
Or thought that other women could have been
As fair as she or e'en as heavenly tall;
But now I want her as a game wants life
To grow into a perfect flower and gain
Perfection - - as a starving man wants food
I want her as my own, my only wife,
To help my manhood's strength to gain
More power through her from perfect womanhood.

November 21, 1886

VI

Yet what is love? It is a simple fool
Who walks a gaol and calls it Paradise,
A magic mirror made of fervid eyes,
Reflecting truth as in the troubled pool
Nature is soon out of all natural rule.
It is a cage for silly butter-flies
To beat their wings against. It is the skies
A baby clutches at - - It is a school
Vanity, to teach
The bitter truth the saddened years attest - -
Of faith that dies upon a woman's breast;
A blushing fruit that ripens out of reach,
A mighty wave that dies upon the beach,
A life all weakness, a mind all unrest.

November 22, 1886

VII

No, that's not love. Love is but love alone,
And laughs at poets and their metaphors.
We say love is like this or that, perforce,
A subtle power, a fire, a dart, -- a tone
Straight from the foot of God's eternal throne
That troubles through all space and strikes the shores
Of Earth within the circuit of its course,
And tells of heaven -- and the earth has gone!
But none the mightiest poets ever told
The all of love. We tread the flowery grove
And pluck sweet fruit of Knowledge free and bold
And say " 'Tis good." But no man ever wove
The all of love in words his pen controlled.
Love is not known but felt. Love is but love.

November 25, 1886

VIII

I walked with her across the shrouded hills,
Her gloved hand resting on my arms the while,
And pressing close to emphasize a smile,
Or make more musical her happy trills
That gushed like wine a bursted skin out spills --
A candid girl in whom there was no guile,
The woman gone. I heard the winds beguile
The laughing waters and spring daffodils --
Should I now ask her? Shall I speak the word?
My heart leaps hot, imagination weaves
A glowing picture of my life's desire
But ah! What bitter sound was that I heard?
The gruesome sighs of winds among dead leaves --
The last faint crackle of a dying fire.

December 1, 1886

IX

She is a queen of most consummate art
If she deceives me by her candid ways
--So soft and winning; yet at times a haze
Seems breaking from the dullness of my heart
And from its vagueness spectres seem to start
That mock my simpleness--and other days
I feel too clearly all her candor says
And know her false. But yet no single part
Of all my trust in her can I abate
When she looks at me with soul-deep surprise
If I suggest it; and, at any rate,
I'll trust her till I know. I do despise
That masque of love that makes love desecrate,
And call that treason which its fears devise.

December 5, 1886

X

Tonight I learned she loved me. And I furled
Her to my heart and life. And then I knew
What that old Hebrew poet meant who drew
The picture of the founding of the world
For all my life's foundations failed and swirled
And rose a-now, and in the deep night's blue
The stars sang, and all earth and Heaven through
The shouts of angels rose and fell and whirled.
The pent-up waves of mighty love burst forth
And rushed throughout the winding coves of space
And bore us with them. Far below, the earth
Sang with the other stars its song apace
And from the East and South and West and North
There gleamed a splendor centring in her face.

December 5, 1886

95

XI

She cannot guess the marvellous peace with which
She fills me, ever-flowing my whole soul
With still deep floods withstanding all control,
Wherein I lose myself in thought so rich
And deep I seem to stand within a niche
Aside with God and see the ages roll
Into eternity - - all strife and dole
Save where I stand alone. The mighty ditch
That guards the fair land of her virgin sweetness
Strong love alone can leap; but He has taken
My hand in His and armed with His completeness
I've made the leap and all else is forsaken;
And I lie buried in her own repleteness
And eat the golden fruit her hand hath shaken.

December 6, 1886

XII

I think I loved her just at first because
Of her mere physical beauty, at whose sight
I felt what rapture is an artist's right
In view of all perfection. Yet I pause
Even now in saying this. Perhaps there was
Some dim suggested beauty of the Infinite,
In proof of which her beauty is the white
Unstained expression - - as a veil of gauze
May be of rarest beauty, yet disclose
The greater beauty that it half conceals
Behind its folds. For I do know there rose
Within me the truth the anchorite feels
When in that deep, ecstatic, frantic state
He walks alone with God within His gate.

XIII

I have communed with but myself alone
On that conglomerate past that has gone by
Walking alone where unseen founts spring high
With Love's great ocean o'er me. But, my own,
Since thou hast come to me, since I have known,
I, a worn traveller wandering desperately,
That one tear-sparkled star within a sky
Else black, hath yearned till it hath shone
And saved me, I give my whole love-life to thee,
Yearning to twine myself with thee as now
I twine my fingers in thy sweet dark hair,
For I so love thee out of all degree
That I would cling to thee as do the fair
White roses love-twined cling around thy brow.

December 13, 1886

XIV

Infinite sweetness of her fair face, pale
As the languid lilies in the heat of noon
That tremble in a tense enraptured swoon
Half-smothered in delight their pains exhale!
Infinite sweetness of her woman's veil
Of womanhood that like the magic moon
Within some fair rose-garden in rose June
Hints beauty that makes other beauty stale!
Infinite sweetness of her heart's appeal
Beating 'gainst mine in iterant unison
Of else unutterable love! I feel
Her soul's still sweetness like a new dawn steal
Within my soul's wide windows till the dawn
Breaks into day and brightens on and on.

December 14, 1886

XV

There dwells a fountain in my heart whose stream
Grows fuller all the more it over-flows
And clearer all the more its 'sturbance grows
And brighter with each gold reflected beam.
Within its bosom mirrored is the gleam
Of a heaven purer than the changing close
Of that we call earth's heaven where the rose
Mantles the lily in a rare esteem.
Ah, sweet! love is that fount and thy white soul
Is . . . .

December 15 - - 21, 1886

98

DATED POEMS
August 30, 1881 to November 20, 1886

TO.............

August 30, 1881

Farewell! Who'd have thought that our late pleasant friendship
　　Would ever result in this untimely end.
　　And to me, oh how sad to ever discover
Such a change in the heart of one once called a friend.

　Your coldness surprised me. I e'en must acknowledge
　　The loss of your friendship is something to me
　　But still as you broke it I've no lamentations
　　But most humbly bow in submission to thee.
　　　If ever in future you have a misgiving
　　That your treatment of me was not truly just
　　Then think of the one you so unjustly censured
And reflect on the days when I once held your trust.
　　Farewell, I regret that you e'er deigned to listen
To the voice of Dame Grundy you said you despised,
　　And you spoke so sincerely that I was deluded
　　And am sorry to find that you apostatized.
Of course, 'tis no more than I could have expected
　　I've proof of your actions as.............

Lines Etc.

Farewell! delightful world, with all thy joys and cares,
　　And all the love which once did bind me here
　　　I go, but in departing have no fears
　　But quite contented leave this pleasant sphere.

　My friends are dear to me. Ah! yes indeed 'tis true
　　I love the few whom Nature gave to me
　Leave-taking will be short, they're now so few
　　Farewell, I wish them joy of what may be.

101

I go, and when in future years my grave they see
I hope 'twill be with longing and regret
They read the tablet to my memory
And drop a tear for him who loves them yet.

October 4, 1881

Portent

Unmeasured oceans 'round me now
Unbounded waves toss high,
Unconquered winds guide on my prow
To waft me to the sky.

In vain I look, in vain I shout;
All calls for aid are vain.
No hand but God's to help me out,
No land but His to gain.

Why do I shrink this fate to meet?
Why trembling do I stand?
Is faith so weak?
Is life so sweet
In this unhappy land?

Oh! for a faith to meet my God
With simple trust and love.
Forget the ills of this poor sod,
In heavenly lands above.

Written in "Mathematics"
October 6, 1882
Hour 11-12 A.M.
Penn. College

For Aye

I love her, I love her,
I cannot tell why
But softly above her
My soul watches nigh.
My thoughts I discover
(What a dreamer am I!)
Always lovingly of her
For whom I would die.

God bless her forever
So noble, so true,
Penelope never
Such constancy knew.--
--And loving thoughts of her
Unguardedly stray
And 'round her they hover
For ever and aye.

November 21, 1883

Woman, Wife And Mother

Woman, wife and mother, these three thou art
Lowly, pure and lovely, in thy humble path
More perfect joy and love and peace untold
And blessed happiness illumes thy course
Than myriads of diadems could confer.
And what unhappy mortal can reveal
The pangs, regrets and heartaches sore and long
Of him who every disappointment meekly bore
For thy sweet sake--and lost the cherished prize.
I love thee! and therefore my song shall rise
Far o'er the shouts of multitudes and dare
To sing thy praises in the face of all
The pride and pomp and vanity of life.

103

And better far for having given my love
To thee without thy love reciprocal
My soul will wing its last long flight
Content, serene and happy with the thought
Of future meeting once and evermore.

Winter of '83

Modern Poetry

Rhyme and Rhythm, Rhyme and Rhythm
Full of artful mechanism
Void of thought hence free from schism
Decomposing like a prism
All poetic organism
Till we hate this horrid rhythm
Till we loathe both rhyme and rhythm
Rhyme and rhythm, rhyme and rhythm
Idiot's play-things, rhyme and rhythm
Woe are ye, oh! rhyme and rhythm.

December 2, 1883

To "Somebody"

What were this barren earth and life and all
What care I for vain honors heaped on me
What tho I have success and fame withal
And have not thee?

I know no thoughts, no actions, which, in sooth
Thou dost not, like a guardian angel guide,
My life were full of purest love and truth
If by thy side.

104

I turn to thee for help when I am weak
And unsuspected thou my strength dost give
I could not the all else besides thee seek
    Without thee live.

Thou sweetest angel and my beacon light
To thee blind Hope persistant lures me on
With thee to triumph thro life's stormy night
    Till break of dawn.

And when while striving on for thy dear sake
We close our lives replete with truest love
My solace be thy trysting kiss to take,
    In realms above.

January 27, 1884

Thurlingian Song

Oh! how can any fate
From thee me separate?
Believe me from my heart I love thee true;
Thou hast so perfectly
Possessed my soul that me
No other can encharm
But thee, but thee.

Respectfully dedicated
to . . . .

Carlisle, April 3, 1884

105

Oh, Wind!

O! fair west wind, whose balmy smiles
Bring peace and gladness to my heart,
Whose fairy touch my soul beguiles
From worldy clamor to depart,

Whose dainty fingers thro my hair
In gentle childish frolic run
Pressing away my life's dull care
With days of rarest halcyon,

I honor thee, I hail thee, sweet,
I rush within thy warm embrace
My noblest offrings at thy feet,
I bring thee for thy loving grace.

When but a child in laughing glee,
I frolicked with thee o'er the dale
Thou wert <u>her</u> friend and thou from me
The confidant of many a tale.

Those childish days, how sweet, how rare,
O Memory saddest of the sad!
When naught remains but breeding care
Oh wind! it almost drives me mad,

For, fair west wind, I tell thee now,
I've never told a soul but thee
These weary eyes and pallid brow
Are all that's left in life to me,

For Wind--e'en now your tender eyes
Are all suffused with diamond tears
And as of old you sympathise
And try to soothe away my fears--

For she whose childhood joys you know,
Whose sunny brow your kiss impressed
Whose eager feet so often drew
By thy soft hand to be caressed,

Grown to sweet womanhood and true
(For whose dear sake I'd gladly die)
--O, Wind, how hard to tell e'en you
Is dead to me for aye, for aye.

May 14, 1884

Ibrahim Bey Tewfik.... A Ballad

Recited June 25, 1884 . . . . . "Junior Exhibition" P. C.

Red as blood in dusty glory sank the sun o'er Egypt's shore--
Down behind the gilded turrets sank as if to rise no more,
Slowly, slowly, fading ever, falling last on Moslem tower--
Red in shame for Egypt's honor, trembling in rebellion's power.

O'er the spires of distant Sinkat, fading in the nearing night,
Fell a hush of painful stillness, calmed the rising clamor's might
And there hovered in the silence of the balmy evening air,
Many a whispered, earnest suppliance--'twas the evening
hour of prayer.

Out upon the dusty level round about the ancient walls
Lay the outlawed troops of treason, waiting for the Signal calls
Breathing deep and sullen hatred with each passion-
quivering breath
Longing eagerly for battle, famished with the thirst of death.

But within that 'leguered city stood a small, heroic band
Trusting for their nation's honor in the Strength of Allah's hand
Tense and grim each stony visage, resolution written there
Bound to win or bound to perish--death or victory to share.

107

Weeks and weeks of weary watching, hoping vainly for relief
  Driven last to desperation tho still trusting to their chief--
    He whose voice had often cheered them, he whose hand
      had often pressed
    Theirs in warm and earnest greeting--Egypt's manliest
      and best,

Now at length resolved to end it--"Men," he firmly, bravely cried,
    "Ye whose blood has stained the desert, fighting by your
      chieftains' side
Ye whose hearts I know are centred in the faith which we believe,
  Follow now for sake of Allah, Freedom, Honor and Khedive;

  Meet the foe--the rebels--meet them, strike with courage
    for the right
Let me not be grieved and humbled by a coward act this night,
If our plan shall be discovered--heave no fainting, cringing sigh--
Strike then valiantly for Egypt, do your uttermost--and die!

In the darkness, never faltring, out the city's gates they went,
  Never casting backward glances to th' abandoned battlement.
All was silent. In the distance gleamed the lights of Osman's camp
Flitting to and fro, with now and then a horse's restless tramp.

In her home in distant Cairo, far away from war's turmoil
Waited Tewfik's little daughter, loveliest flower of Egypt's soil,
  Pacing nervously her chamber, mind intent on father's fate,
  Naught could calm her heart's tumultuous longing; she could
    only wait.

Ah! but hark, the camp's astir now, what a rush and roar of arms;
  How they pour from every quarter at the signal-gun's alarms.
  Tewfik cries--"Our plan's discovered, but, remember," then
    he turns,
  And a glow of heavenly glory bright upon his pale face burns.

Now they meet, see! how he towers, head and shoulders 'bove
    them all,
Cheering on to death the comrades who around him thickly fall,
    Short but fierce the battle rages; overpowered every man
Fights till lost, a very demon - - Then they die as brave man can.

When the sun rose on the morrow, glorious, radiant and bright,
    For did Egypt's sacred honor saved by Ibrahim that night
Dead he lay, his comrades near him, earth and all its hopes forgot
But for them what <u>son of freedom</u> could desire a happier lot?

Tewfik Bey! thy name we honor! Midst the storied heroes dwell,
    Thou whose heroism never can all history excel,
Giant heart! the faint with longing for the loved ones safe at home
    Never from thy path of Duty, let thy slightest action roam!

And that sad-eyed little daughter, now disconsolate for thee
'Reft of Hope and all earth's pleasure in her loving constancy,
Gained at Sinkat what shall ever-as it rings from age to age,
Bless <u>her</u> name in hallowed Tewfik's - - <u>Honor's noblest heritage</u>.

P. G. June 7, 1884

Love--An Allegory

One day when dancing sunbeams kissed the air,
And whispering leaves at light flirtations played,
    Love sought and found a pretty maiden fair,
And in her snowy bosom would have stayed.

But no! the maiden with a cool disdain,
Careless and cruel and too worldly-wise,
Said, "Trouble not, come when Life's pleasures wane."
Love, quickly turning from her, elsewhere tries.

Years after when he chanced to pass that way
She then the suppliant was - - "O, Love," she cried,
"Love, pass me not, stay with me but a day,
And let the blessed memory e'er abide."

109

Pitying, he glanced: then on again he sped.
She, hopeless, joyless, loveless, soon was dead.

July 12, 1884

Lines On My 19th Birthday

August 15, 1884

Today my years are numbered.
With Hopes, with Fears encumbered,
With Smiles, with Tears encumbered,
Today,
My soul hath yet but slumbered,
But waketh now for aye.

Full many a boyish notion
Of Life's love-giving potion
Of Love's life-giving potion
Today,
Are ghosts of a lost devotion
That flicker and fade away.

The Angels that wafted o'er me
From a land far, far before me,
From a land of Love before me,
Today,
To Truth and to Beauty restore me,
Lisp gently their Hope alway.

From the day of ill-fate they met me
The Demons that always beset me
The Devils of Hell that beset me
Today,
Are plotting, are swearing to get me
To keep me and damn me at bay.

110

Great One - - to Thy care I commend me
From Death, from destruction defend me
From the Death that is Nothing defend me
Today,
But to Death that means Glory befriend me
And near Thee and with Thee to stay.

For Life let my object be ever
From the trust of my mistress never
From the trust of the Beautiful never
To stray.
Let Art be my mistress forever
And I but her servant for aye - -

Life

See 'neath yon oak on yonder grassy knoll
An aged man alone and sadly sits,
The weight of years hangs heavy on his soul
The night-owl vainly hoots him as she flits.

Long years have added silver to his hair
And furrowed lines on his once placid brow
The gloomy witnesses of sin are there
And mask the majesty of manhood now.

The stars come out and dance around the moon
The lover to his lady's window goes
The crickets hymn their chirping cheerful tune
And all the earth is settled in repose.

August 1884

You

Loveliness of heart, of mind, of soul,
All sundered in Earth's wildernesses grew,
Till she produced in one most lovely whole
The unity of loveliness in <u>you</u>.

August 1884

Retrospect

(Rondel)

Ah! dear! that I, a barren stalk am left
And she, the lily, gone long years to sleep!
Ah! wretched life, of all sweet thought bereft
Save sad sweet thought of he and youth, I weep,
--And Time laughs mockingly and the memories steep
My heart in aching as to weep were theft--

Ah! dear! That I, a barren stalk, am left
--And she, the lily, gone long years to sleep!
Would that those years did off my shoulders heft
And I might on one solemn June-eve peep--
She, I, sequestred: Once again her deft
Cool fingers o'er my heated forehead sweep--
Dear heart! That I alone and old am left
And she, the lily, gone long years to sleep.

October 27, 1884
Penn. College
Room 42

Poem For The Class-Day Exercises Of The Class Of '85

Tuesday, June 23, 1885

Dear friends, it is just that I could not refuse
That I draped for this meeting my tricksy old muse
She was sick, and I feared that she'd never revive
Till I whispered "You're wanted for old '85."

112

She was sick, you'll admit it, I think, when I'm done
But consider, she's out on a frolic, "for fun."
She has stept from her palace of classical wealth
And is taking a ramble, this evening, for health.

Oh! Pallas Athene, forgive me, I pray.
Forgive me this shockingly jocular lay--
Forgive us if aught of sound rev'rence we lack.
Forgive our dear critics and bless the whole pack.

I give you our class as she nears graduation
All hail to the best set of men in creation--
I greet you with joy. You greet me, I know it
As that worst of all bores, the confounded class-poet.

Well! Well! if there's one here who hears out my ditty
One friend, if he hail from the country or city,
I'm content. If he wishes, I'll meet him yet later
And quaff a full glass to our old alma-mater.

"Ah? Precisely. I see it. You all want to say
That a tear is too sad and a laugh is too gay."
But, my class, at this meeting all sadness be banished
We're united: we're free. Our troubles have vanished.

We are wise. Why, my friends, the amount that we know
Would frighten you all, 'twould astonish you so!
Our Professors, they're around here somewhere, a half-score
Keep well in the back-ground, at thought of our love.

Ha! ha! We have got them. They're awed at our learning.
They know well the fires they have kindled are burning.
They know that they're distanced. We don't hesitate or
Stop once to say it. I cite you the "Senator."

There's one of us here, only one, I regret it,
Who boasts in a way that you'll never forget it.
Who boasts, --I imagine when none else are by
He makes this proud boast with a sort of a sigh--

113

That he never in all his collegiate relations
E'er found any fault with the wise regulations
Or violated ever to his or your knowledge
A single good Rule of this Singular College.

Ex uno - - what's the rest? If I could I'd get that in - -
It's surely no sin to forget, now, one's Latin
Well! One's memory's elastic. I meant every man
Of our class should be judged by our whiskered friend "Dan".

There's another one here just in passing I'll mention,
- - I pray you, my friends, give this fact your attention - -
Who never has yet in the course of his living
Been caught in the fashionable vice of wine-bibing.

He's ne'er touched a drop. He's a dude. He's a dandy
He's had trouble with gamins. The law he found handy
He arrested a few. He gave them a "filler."
Who is it? You've guessed him - - our friend "Toughy" Miller.

There's a fourth - - he's a tremendous man for athletics
His health is not good so he takes dietetics.
He's a student, but yet it's all "under the rose" - -
But find me the equal of genial "Nose."

These are only a few of us. You see our variety
I could cite you such points to quite a satiety.
I'll spare you. I know, from the smile on your faces
You're very well pleased with my word for their graces.

We've jokes of our own now. Since we're out of College
We laugh a great deal at the thought of our Knowledge.
Our Professors were witty. We laughed, then, alack!
Oh! Why did we laugh at the jokes they would crack?

Oh! tell me, ye shades of our classical friends!
Oh! tell me, ye jokers, we'd fain make amends!
Oh! tell me, ye walls! Who knows? Who knows?
These jokes should have lulled the best man to repose.

114

Well! well! tempus fugit. Let us glance at that Past
When ten-pin balls rolled and tin horns blew their blast
Let us call back to mind that old Freshman foray
When we filled up the chapel with arm-fuls of hay.

How long has it been since they all tried to cramp us
By making us <u>play</u> for a day on the campus.
'Tis not hard to recall how that small scheme of Doctor's
Revealed us that night when we tied in the Proctors.

Ex uno, again. They sought us like ferrets
And for all our sweet pranks they gave us demerits.
'Twas but fair: for, of course, when <u>our</u> race was run
'Twas natural that they should want <u>their</u> share of fun.

Let us look to the Future. We are great men all through
We'll teach these wise ancients what moderns can do.
Our blessing be with them. Hurrah! we are off!
--Kind friend! how I thank you for giving that cough.

'Twas the signal to stop. I shall take but a minute
To add a few lines that 'twere well to put in it--
They're but short, and I know when you hear their allusion
Your minds will see light in this mass of confusion.

"Bibamus ad classem vocatam "The Boys."
Et eorum tutores, eorum "joys"
"Et floreant, valeant, vigeunt tam,
Non Jupiter ipse enumeret quam"--

When Comes The Hour

When comes the hour to every heart
When, crushed, the proud Life-flower
Lie bleeding-oh! what hopes depart,
    When comes the hour.

What miserable thoughts devour,
What dark unfathomed terrors start,
While ominous, threatening life-clouds lower.

Nor Nature's charms nor rarest art
Can stay the archer's power,
We stagger on; but sticks the dart
    When comes the hour.

Yale Divinity School
December 2, 1885

Written on-board a train

Yale Divinity School - circa 1885

Photo Courtesy of the Yale University Library

To Bob Hardinge

Dear Bob, old friend of mine,
How do you do?
A thousand hearty grips I send,
And one full glass of wine
I drink to you
This wintry night.
Another party sips, my friend,
And other glad eyes shine
And cheeks grow bright
In these old cozy nooks where you and I
When late bells rang
And those old prosy books were all cast by
Clasped hands and sang.
It is their right;
For what is youth if it be not free
And who are we
That time should bring us to such vain despite
To quiz their right?
Ah, Bob, we would
Not, if we could.

II

Oh! no, 'twas not a sob
You heard, dear Bob,
I did but cough
And that that makes me wink
I know you think
Must be a tear for those old days gone by,
But, no, you're "off"
'Twas something in my eye.
You see, on nights like this
I cannot tell it

With half the productive art
It needs.
But speeds
My time and I must on
Those dear old days, alas, are gone.

III

Rememberest thou our mid-night walks
And those old serenades
With other friends we used to sing?
Well, well, rememberest too, the talks
We had with graceful maids,
And how sometimes on those night walks
Our trophies home we'd bring?
Here's to our dear old room,
Forty-two!
No life of groan or gloom
E'er make it blue!
Joy be its doom!
And heavy be its air with glad perfume!

But here
Bob dear
I sing a song for both our lives
And profit by it both we may and will
And if our wine
Grow increase while all thrives
Or if it spill
A smiling face be always yours and mine.

IV

1

Let life be all gladness,
Be banished all sadness,
Be vanished all badness.
And if there come sorrow
Let none of us borrow
Sad face of tomorrow.

2

If wine-cups be filling
Or if they be spilling
Let each heart be willing.
And when comes sad warning
All slothfulness scorning
Be ready for morning.

3

Then joy be our portion
Let no vile abortion
Or savage distortion
Of truth e'er be given;
And as we have striven
So be our chains riven.

The years, dear Bob, may bring us weal or woe
But as we go
I hold you out my hand and yours
I take and hold
So old, so old.

V

This world moves on, but moves remorseless slow.
'Tis we who come and pass;
And while our fount of life out pours
This grey old world, alas;
Rolls on in grim serenity of mass,
Nor cares.
Sing out
Ring out
Fling out
The hope of one who dares.
My candle flickers and my minutes are but few
I close those hasty lines
With my friendly benisons on what e'er you do.
I'm well, my life confines
But little variation.
In sweet expectation
I await
A letter from you at an early date;
And remain

As in the days of old, even now as then,
In sunshine or in rain
Your old friend Bren.

Chloe

You shun me, Chloe, like the fawn
That seeks its trembling mother, on
The far-off hills,
In silly fear of winds and wood,
For if Spring's nestlings break the hush
On leaves preluding wealth of good
Or lizard part the black-berry bush

With fear it thrills;
But, sweet, I follow, not as beast
To crush thee when thou knowest least;
But beg thee, quit thy mother's side,
And be my own, my bride.

July 26, 1886

✦ ✦

In Reply To A Gift Of Flowers

These flowers that come from you to me,
With all your loving care about them,
I know are simply meant to be
The sign of what I know without them,
Yet still another sense I see,
And have no doubt or wish to doubt them.

"Who would be worthy of the trust
A loving heart unchanged reposes,
Should prove it by his living just
As simply as a flower uncloses,
For one true heart is more than dust
And vanity of faded roses!

The love that taught me what it is
To gauge my fealty by my living
Shall ever, by my hope of bliss,
Be strength for undefeated striving,
No other wreath be mine than this
With your dear hand to bless the giving!

August 14, 1886

On Coming Of Age

Ah! hopes of manhood! No one knows
What strange fulfillment they shall find.
God grant me, through all joys and woes,
    A fair, contented mind.

Today Life lifts my face to his
--His face I ne'er so truly scanned.
How worn and sad and scarred it is.
    How fever-stained and tanned!

Yet what rare sweetness in his eyes,
So deep and dark and strange of hue!
They seem to gleam of Paradise,
    They tell me he is true.

I grasp his hard hand firmer still,
I feel a slight responsive press.
O Life, be rugged as you will,
    But leave me one caress.

O lead me not in ways that go
Dishonor's arrant province in,
Nor let me write my name in snow,
    Nor share my couch with sin.

O, Keep me in the plain I tread,
All-scorning little things and base,
High ever every earth-born dread,
    And worthy of my place.

High thoughts and aspirations fine
Today with earnest purpose hold,
Since youth and life and love are mine
    What fancy is too bold?

Ah, dreams of manhood! Heaven knows
What strange fulfillment they shall find,
God grant me through all joys and woes,
A fair contented mind.

August 15, 1886

Palingenesis

As the sun went down, and the day was going,
I came from the dim, still chamber of prayer,
And the stream of my life that was darkly flowing
Seemed nearing the ocean men call despair.

At last had my heart grown faint with its yearning,
And I loved not life and I feared not death.
I was learning--ah, end of my youth!--I was learning
That life is a waiting and joy is a breath.

Soon the sun was down, and the night wind blew me
Sweet scent from the lily-starred heaven of leas,
And a calm that was vocal with promise drew me
Far on in the beautiful darkness - and peace.

All the night I wandered until morn the maiden,
Came tripping along in the path I trod;
And she kissed me--low as I was and laden--
And I kissed her again, and her kiss was God.

New Haven, October 2, 1886

*Varies in 2nd, 3rd, and 4th stanzes from published poem
which follows.*

124

Palingenesis

As the sun went down, and the day was going,
I came from the dim, still chamber of prayer,
And the stream of my life that was darkly flowing
Seemed nearing the ocean men call despair.

As my heart grew faint with its hapless yearning,
I clung not to life, and I shrank not from death,
I was learning--ah! end of my youth--I was learning
That life is a waiting and joy is a breath.

Soon the sun was down, and the night wind blew me
Sweet scent from the lily-starred heaven of leas,
And a sense like a mother-heart pleaded, and drew me
Far on in the shadowy darkness-and peace.

I roamed all the night till the angel of morning,
Spread his white, fair wings o'er the way that I trod;
And he opened my eyes to his beauty, adorning
All earth, air, and sky, with the goodness of God.

Copied from Penna. College Monthly
Gettysburg, Pa. February, 1887

Manuscript found.

A Rose From The Bride's Bouquet

Velvety, beautiful, chaste,
A rose from the bride's bouquet,
Fair as the bosom it graced,
Frail as the veil it displaced.
Tremblingly hurried away
The bride and her retinue gay
Forsaking the garlanded rooms
And nothing but fragrant perfumes
And I, in the solitude stay--
With a rose from the bride's bouquet.

125

Out with the flare of the gas,
Let the fond memories stray
Back to the sweet little lass
Bounding away in the grass.
Culling bright flowers in play,
All unaware of the day
Love should make captive her heart,
Let the old memories start;
Alone in the solitude gray
With a rose from the bride's bouquet.

Beat high in thy joy, little heart,
Shine out like the sun to the day,
Close-pressed to the breast whose thou art,
Beat high to thy soul's counter-part,
Love commands, little heart; obey.
For thee, in the darkness, I pray.
Un-thought-of, un-minded, forget - -
Dreaming of youth I have met,
Yet finding sufficient repay
In a rose from the bride's bouquet.

November 18, 1886

My Sweet

The brook-let sings my love and me a merry, merry tune,
As we sit close together in the sunny afternoon,
And so I think and say
To her this perfect day,
My sweet,
Your words complete
The sound of the brooklet at your feet.

126

The skies are blue as sapphire above my love and me,
They seem to gleam on purpose for such a pair as we,
And so I think and say
To her this perfect day,
My sweet,
Your eyes complete
The blue of the skies they're turned to greet.

The roses glow with passion upon the trembling bush,
They're like the sky's last flushes before the evening hush,
And so I think and say
To her this perfect day,
My sweet,
Your cheeks complete
The glow of the roses they repeat.

Two birds as red as poppies come flitting down the breeze.
My love calls softly to them. They vanish through the trees.
And so I think and say
To her this perfect day,
My sweet,
Your lips complete
The red of the birds they would entreat.

My love is young and slender, her heart is mine alone,
I think the sun in heaven for her more brightly shone,
And so I think and say
To her this perfect day,
My sweet,
You are complete
And all fair things your charms repeat.

November 20, 1886

127

MISCELLANEA

After The Manner Of Man
The Poet

We let him live neglected and obscure
Called him inane and his work absurd
Killed him at last - - still young and heavenly pure - -
And scorned the eternal message of his word!

They give him <u>now</u> the cant amens of praise
Raise to his name vain - glorious scars of stone,
Quote him, forsooth, and say the heavens blaze
The brighter for the star whose light has flown;

Print him immortal, dedicate him great,
Rant of the pride his purblind nation feels,
Don all the virtues guilt may simulate,
And crush out conscience under golden wheels.

Oh, shame - - that should see genuis all too late
And slave with words their flesh-wounds of remorse
As if 'twere noble and a thing to prate
To starve a brother and to feast his corse.

Great God of Truth! when will they learn to know
How clear the water ere they break the fount,
When will they greet the glorious morning glow
And see its beauty when the sun shall mount?

To The Spirit Of Art

Thou art more fair than far-famed Rosamund,
O, subtle singer to my inmost life,
That linkest me with thee; thou art the wife
Of all my purest fancy-chilled or sunned
Upon the shore of that unknown profund

131

Whence song takes wing aloft, or, like a knife,
Cuts deep within the unfathomed waves whose strife
Brings saddened thought of sweetness moribund;

Sometimes I see thee, gossamer-veiled in sheen,
Resplendent as the rosy Morn when dews
Distill their diamonds where her feet have been;
But most I only hear thee. - - Ah! refuse
Me not the grace my straining heart hath seen,
- - More wifely trust, more lingering interviews.

A Castle In Spain

I dwelt in a castle full high,
All complete in a sunshiny plain,
A happy young prince then was I,
Who rejoiced in a glorious reign,
I knew neither sorrow nor pain,
And won everything by a dash
But alas! my young hope was soon slain
- - My castle came down with a crash.

'Twas never my nature to cry
So (I sha'n't stop just now to explain.)
I built me another near by
A castle of rose and champagne
But my new usurpation was vain
For King and his kingdom w'd clash
As neither had grace to abstain.

Then I built me a spire to the sky,
A love-colored castle in Spain
But (I couldn't exactly tell why!)
The queen simply fled the domain.

132

At first I was slightly profane
And might have done something quite rash
But I soon learned my ire to contain.

Prince, be advised, to be plain
Your visions of youth are all flash
I should not have been now in your train.
But . . . .

◄§ §►

Her Beauty

We strolled at even on a pebbly beach
We rested in the balmy bracing air
And there I revelled in the snowy reach
Of her unrivaled bosom. In her hair
Blacker than blackest midnight gleamed a star
Of pure, serenest pearls, which half uphold
And half released the glowing radiant mass.
Downward it fell around her glorious neck
And fell upon her breast's majestic swell
And loving lingered. Oh, with what a joy
I drank her beauty in! Her dreamy eyes
Brown as the hazel's softly beamed
In conscious purity on me. How could I
Look and look unmoved, and not be lifted higher --
And purer, nobler feel myself to be
In presence of this living breathing sprite?
Her face was lovely and her supple form
Pliant and graceful as the timid fawn.

The bright sunlight in the darkness of my mental loneliness and physical indifference - - (scribbled on a scrap of paper, on which over and over is many times repeated the name, L. B. Brenner)

133

A Notion

I don't know if it's so, but the truth seems to grow
And the notion is rather uncommon;
As I sit here tonight it seems to my sight
That the man in the moon is a woman.

And I'll tell you what's more, she is old and she's poor
And unmarried and deeply dejected
And for fear we should grow quite too knowing, you know,
Her face that we see is reflected,

For the moon is her mirror in which just to cheer her
When callers come rarely or flee her.
This little old maid (she's vain, I'm afraid)
Fakes very long looks -- so we see her --

And the clouds seem to be her pin-cushions, you see,
And the stars that are merrily peeping
Are only the bright shining pin-heads stuck tight
In the cushion for very safe-keeping.

And to prove this mean-while, just consider her smile
Such a smile for a man is uncommon;
And that's why it seems as she brightens and beams
That the man in the moon is a woman.

Unfinished Poem

One night -- God knows how bitter-sweet
The memory of that night now seems!
I woke from rosiest of dreams
To face the worst and meet.

Ay, meet! for who was I that I
Should dare aspire where nobler men
Had failed? Could I be true again,
Vile one who lived a lie?

How could she love me - - she whose heart
No faintest breath of sin had fanned?
So pure, so good. God never planned
    A thing of finer part.

    A noble woman is God's work.
    A noble man is woman's. You
Who know what woman's love can do,
    What mighty powers lurk
Beneath the . . . . E. I. Brenner (F. B. S.)

    Beneath the subtle outer cloak
    Of innocence, You understand
    I dared to touch her lovely hand
    In dreams from which I woke.

But when my sorrow she bethought
My scarlet sins were shriven. She
    In sweet surrender gave to me
    The love I humbly sought.

Remorse
Death In Child-Birth - - - -

If I had known! O woe the bitterest
That ever followed man's unthinking nod!
O hell of hells! O soul of all unrest!
O dear, dead love in lucent depth of sod
Revealed - - Pity! - - Scorn me not, my best,
Turn thy dear coffined face away - - O God,
    If I had known!

I killed her - - cured me, foul and most unjust!
Killed her but loved her - - Loved her? Aye, how much
Look on my face and tell! Distrust! Distrust!
Will none believe me? O, her cold, cold touch!
In hell's eternal living fire I'm thrust
There is no hell but this! Her hands I clutch!
Great God, If I had known!

Louise

Strange! how thought will wander so.

Weary year is growing old,
Strange, Louise,
And the winter winds are cold
Oh, Louise,
But your heart, I know, has nought of
All the storm and strife I wot of
and I think (I've often thought) of
You, Louise.

Years have wandered since we met,
Years, Louise,
Tears have made our eye-lids wet,
Tears, Louise,
And tonight my eyes are mistful
And I seem to see a wistful
Tearful vision of a tristful
Wan Louise.

But I shake the fancies from
Me, Louise,
For the odd romance is dumb
Now, Louise,
Though you missed me sadly, sorely,
One whole day wept undemurely
Kissed me passionately, purely
Last, Louise.

But I dream your eyes are bright
As, Louise,
They were that parting night
Then Louise,
And their liquid grace is gladdening
Him a year ago 'twas maddening
And <u>my</u> heart alone is saddening
Now, Louise.

Was it you or I to blame,
Sweet Louise
That the glad day never came,
Sweet Louise.
Did we love each other truly
Think you, or did wisdom duly
Regulate our hearts unruly
Sweet Louise.

Just this hour I love but you,
Dear Louise,
Years have left me but us two,
And, Louise,
Since my love has nought of value
Let my memory sweet enthrall you
And this last sad time I'll call you
My Louise.

A Sufficient Reason

"Dear Hal," she writes, "I cannot come
I am so very, very sorry
The violets - - (I send you some) - -
Are making all the meadow starry!"

"Remember how they were last year
The day I kissed you when we wandered?
The violets again are here
The kisses, Hal, have all been squandered."

"And so by way of kind return
For your most flattering invitation
I send you these that you may learn
The vanity of osculation."

"For flowers are constant - - some I know
We both hold highly dear and tender
And, Hal, these flowers will ever show
The good intention of the sender."

(By Jove, the girl is changing much,
I never thought her sentimental.
Is this effusion truly such
Or only - - simply - - accidental?)

"Oh, yes! My reason I forgot,
I'm much excited, flustered, hurried,
I'd love to come (the dear old spot!)
But, Hal, tonight I'm to be married."

How Love Came And Went

He came with springtime,
He went with summer.
'Twas truly kingtime
My hour-and-my-time-
O happy comer
He came

He came full featly
(He went with summer)
He sighed full sweetly
He vowed full neatly
O simple comer
He came

He went full quickly
(He came no slower)
His heart was sickly
His roses prickly,
O sad <u>wise</u> goer
He went.

Nonsense

What though you laugh at woman's fame
With scoffing and derision
Can't you recall some maiden's name
Who like a fleeting vision
Came o'er your life? ('Tis just the same
Now.) With mild submission
You e'en obeyed her every wish and word
And tho't it lucky if your prayer was heard.

The Fay's Ransom

A little foot-print in the sand
A fairy walking on the strand
Left it there and ran away
Humming a fairy roundelay.
Away o'er hill and dale she sped
Till night the moon three times had wed
And reached at last her fairy home
Then tarried there ne'er more to roam,
For e'en as fairy laws decree
What fay so wretched e'er shall be
As on earth's bosom to impress
Her feet through careless awkwardness
Shall ne'er stray forth! but day to day
Shall toil within: O luckless fay!

But earth so loved that tiny mark
That wind nor wave nor ages dark
Could 'rase or even mar the sight
Of that sweet idyl of delight.

Ages and ages passed and oh,
The spinx's riddle puzzled so
The sweet ephemerals as to meet
That feet print with their pearly feet.
E'en Cinderella tried and failed
And myriads of maidens quailed
Before the arduous task till thou
With timid grace and modest brow
O fair co-ordinate of love - -
O radiant vision from above - -
Filled the footprint in surprise
That we should let our wonder rise
So freely to our lips. That day
The footprint were itself away
And once more sped in artless play
The fleeting steps of the ransomed fay.

140

Unchanging

I sing a simple song I know
And do not aim at strong effects,
But truth will ever stronger grow
And all the love that can will flow
Into these simple song-collects.

Long strolls through wood-land avenues
And thoughts exchanged in sympathy
And lingerings long o'er dying views,
She, sweetest view of all to me,
Unchanging in the changing hues.

My Wife

To one dear friend whose love is such
As made me braver knowing her
To live my life not over-much
Inclined to doubt - - a hungerer

For food which comes not soon or late
Till God His wonder-mind reveal
And show in that Infinite fate
The simple Reason of His Will.

But living as I can the best
And truest to myself and all
With faith my guiding-beacon lost
My wayward foot step slip and fall,

And knowing love is love, content
To rest in love, forever-more,
And trusting all in life is meant
To be worth striving, living for, - -

141

To her my saddened being turns,
In her my weary heart finds rest,
For her my lonely being yearns,
In her I call my hearth stone blessed.

With her I know the purest joy
With her, the happiest of life,
And even Grief has some alloy
Shared with the friend of friends, my wife.

A Prayer.....Unfinished

Angels guard him day and night,
With him still though out of sight
One his dream wife, the other
Gentle, tender, loving mother.

Always turning.............

On Christmas-Eve

Hark! the bells are ringing,
Peace, good-will out-flinging,
All the air is singing
Sweetly with their chime;
Pure and clear their voice is,
Hushed the day's loud noise is,
Smiling night rejoices
With their merry rhyme.

Banish woe and sadness,
Banish wrong, 'tis madness.
Hope and love and gladness
Ring the happy bells,

The Smithsburg Lutheran Church in Winter

Sketch drawn by Keith Snow

Out with pain and sorrow
Let the nations borrow
Brave heart of tomorrow,
Still their music swells.

On the calm air stealing,
How they pour, revealing
All the joy that's pealing
From their throbbing hearts.
Ringing loud and louder,
Ringing proud and prouder,
With what depth endowed are
Thoughts their music starts!

Christ, our lord in Heaven,
Christmas Morn was given,
All despair was riven,
From that happy day,
Earth, thy debt confessing,
Take thee of his blessing,
From thy gloom egressing,
Trust and hope for aye.

A Revelation

Life is philosophy. Year after year
I wasted youth's fair promise in the schools.
I rhapsodized on love,
But measured it along with other fools
Only as they who seek love's daily food
In self-love can. Poor weary tools
Doing they know not what of ill or good.

I traveled many lands. My rockless course
- Reaction from the warping, stiffened strain - -
Bore me to all the haunts of shame and vice - -
A gilded, fashionable high-priced chain
Shackling all truth. Rose-colored, warm and sweet
Its flowers were but deathly and at last I fled
Seeking some rest for weariness replete.
It was as though all good in me were dead.

A Poet's Prelude

As one who wakes from sleep and knows not if
His puzzled eyes are ope to night or noon
While scented, psalming wind hastes on my skiff
I lie bewildered 'neath the dying moon.
My soul is lost to ought of life and death
I know not, care not if I die or live
The soft, the oft repeated lappings of the wave
Seem echoes of a grave
And faint, the plaint of Philomela's breath
In sounds more sweet than airs aeolic give
Croons out a shadow-song that saith
"I hymn thee, stranger, of the death of Death."
Her voice seems now my own sad soul that sings
On spotless out-stretched, universal wings,
Sublime, God-sent,
And blind to all the littleness life brings
Sees but the spheric poetry of things,
Mellifluent
As Orphic music that or came or went
Making Death Life and Life incontinent.

A subtle change comes over my frail beat
And Argo-like it seems to float and float
No more at random, but by my soul's song
Ravished and borne obedient along - -

No more at random, yet in no known order
For my soul wanders as a free-willed bird,
Traversing that unseen, celestial border
Where songs are sung that no man ever heard.
Ah! that full hour when beauty evercomes
That poignant hour when sweets untold are told
When love of love in heaven-born breezes hums,
When love is new and life and death are old.
And now I float upon that silver sea
In dreaming of a dream.

Waffed now fast, now slow and painfully
Again swift as bird-flights gleam,
Touching a shore of gladness and of hope
Where fond heart nestle to strong arms that ope
And love rules all the land.

Know you that land, that joy-laden land
Where love-flowers blossom and blow
Where bird songs are calling, and rising and
Falling in eloquent strains that we know
Where shy shadows linger with beckoning finger
O'er heaven and ocean and land
And mild moonlight quivers and shimmers and shivers
Where billows are kissing the strand

Where happiness flutters each rose-word love utters
Straight down at the loved one's feet
And fond eyes are spelling the love that is telling
From eyes never made for deceit?
Know you that land?
Still on my soul to other, sadder shores
Where hope is dead and woe comes all unsought
And all the balm the song of songs outpours
Is but "Hereafter" and "This life is nought."

Know you that land of woe
Where lost love cries?
Where wrecked hearts ever go
With sighs, with sighs?

Where birds glad songs are stilled
Or rise in vain;
Where love's bright wine is spilled
In pain, in pain?
Know you that land?

A post once to us
Preluded softly thus
Then breaking from his song
Lest that it grew too long
Sang the brief tale I tell
And ceasing song no more,
And simply said, " 'Tis well."

Life And I

In the fair night the solemn hours glide by
And Life and I sit thinking of our past.
Weary we both are, sad and somewhat shy,
Like anguished lovers, tete-a-tete at last,
Life holds my hand in his. I never try
To hide from him the luckless die I cast.
In the fair night the solemn hours glide by
And Life and I sit thinking of our past.

We've had a faithful journey -- he and I
And no misfortune turned his face aghast
Dear friend! We're almost home, 'tis nigh, 'tis nigh,
And back thou takest thy freedom long held fast
In the fair nights . . . .

147

Love God

"Love God", she says, "love me"
And tears in her sweet eyes swim-
Having her, can my faith grow dim
And can I, open-eyed, not see?
--Love her and not love Him?

The Singer of Sorrow

The long-silent singer of sorrow is singing again,
There's a rush of the wind down the river, half-drowning his pain,
There's a gleam of a light all about him - a terrible stain -
Will he ever explain, do you think? Will he ever explain?

Do you see there; he's hanging his head out - - far out in the night,
Is he mad? Or is it only a belated traveller in sight?
They said he was ill; he is better. I tell you I'm right
He is singing the strangeness of sorrow - - and singing with might.

The Unfinished Prayer

My little sister, golden-haired,
With eyes all laughter, bubbling over,
And feet a fairy might have dared
Play truant with in fairy clover,
Aweary of her busy day,
Kneels softly down to pray.

She folds the little dimpled hands;
The snowy, rose-leaf lids she closes.
Meanwhile the mother by her stands
To help the little lisper's pauses;
And gently steals the evening air
To catch the murmured prayer.

148

A pause, --- Then from the baby lips
Fall two sweet words her mother taught her -
"Dad bees" -- Another pause. - Then slips
The mother's arm about her daughter;
Then such a weary sigh, and deep,
   - And Golden-hair's asleep.

O, little sister, angels heard
The prayer thy lips refused expression,
And keep it, every golden word,
For thee, a life-long intercession.

God grant, when age has lined thy brow,
   Thy heart be pure as now.

Song Of The Orthodox Poet

I wonder if the time is near
My landlord wants his reckoning;
 I wonder if I've much to fear
From creditors' unmanly sting;
I wonder if this mail will bring
A trifle for my empty purse;
I'm wonder-wonder -- wondering,
I wonder who'll accept my verse.

I wonder if this bottled beer
Is good for health -- or anything;
 I wonder if Miss Vere de Vere
Will like my rondeau to her ring;
 I wonder if from Cupid's wing
I'd pluck a pun, I'd do much worse;
Or would I no more need to sing
I wonder who'll accept my verse?

149

I wonder where I'll be next year,
I wonder where the following;
I wonder when there will appear
My last year's rhapsody on Spring;
I wonder if 'twould be the thing
To heap on destiny a curse;
I wonder what the fates will fling;
- - I wonder who'll accept my verse.

Envoy

I wonder-peasant, priest or king,
What fond, delusive hopes you nurse; - -
But - - mostly to this one I cling,
I wonder who'll accept my verse.

The Proposal

The sun was sinking in the West
Behind the dimpled hills
He seemed to linger on their breast
To move them with his trills.

The day had been most fair and fine
Full sunshine, little shadow,
My heart was full of Madeline
As I walked in the meadow.

I strolled along the shady way,
Where she, I felt, had been
I watched the same blithe birds at play
Which she, I thought, had seen.

I plucked the flowers from the bush
Which she, perhaps, had kissed,
I kissed them in the evening hush,
I pressed them to my breast.

150

I was but young and life to me
Seemed less of earth than heaven,
I cared not for the great to be
Nor thought of fond hopes riven.

The world and all to me were nought,
I loved her--that was all.
And love had all my spirit caught
And held my soul in thrall.

I wandered in the twilight mild,
And dreamed of Madeline.
Sometimes she seemed a charming child
Awaiting to be mine.

And then again a woman she
Repelling my address,
And girt about with dignity,
Yet charming, ne'er the less.

I know not which I thought the more
Enchanting to my mind--
To see her stately, proud and frore,
Or simple, sweet and kind.

I loved her--that alone I know
I'd never questioned why--
The sun had kissed the hills of blue
His last warm kiss good-bye.

And then I saw her proud young head
Across the dimpled hills,
And heard the song she sang, and said
"The birds have taught her trills."

I met her where the fields of green
Were verging to the wood,
Amidst the scented eglantine
That blossomed where she stood.

She stood, the fairest maid, I ween,
That ever man had found,
Her little feet were barely seen
Just peeping from the ground.

Her two white hands she held me out
I gathered in my own
And kissed them 'fore she turned about
Or knew what I had done.

Her lips, her hands, her eyes, her hair
Were thrilling all my soul,
I kissed her red, red lips and then
I found my words control.

I asked her would she be my wife;
I loved but her, I said.
A doubt within me sprang to life
An instant, and was dead.

She hesitated ere she gave
Her little trembling "Yes,"
While o'er her features flushed a wave
Of sweet-unwillingness.

The tears her dear eyes held were yet
Half-struggling to be free.
They fell, and all her trust was set
Forevermore in me.

I know not if the angels knew
The heights we soared among.
I only know our love was true,
And that our hearts were young.

I know not if the angels went
In envy of us then,
But envy we had none to vent
On angels or on men.

Mirage

She sits in her chair by the window-side,
Where the scent of the wood-bine lingers,
With her hair all down in a wavy tide
To her tightly-clasped fingers.
- She sits with her blue eyes opened wide.

She looks too sad for a new-made bride,
So sad 'twere near unhuman.
She scarcely knows what a sigh she sighed,
(O, crushed and suffering woman!)
But it buried deep the love that died.

Soft-as a rose-leaf cleaves the air,
Sad - - beyond all relieving,
It whispered the birth of a long despair,
The death of a short deceiving.
- O, heart but to God alone laid bare!

She dreams of the love-land nevermore,
Her path is the path of duty;
A wife with sadder eyes than of yore,
And the ghost of a former beauty.
- What hope have the burdened years in store?

Part I

Miriam

One day in summer when the busy town
Lay chafing, like a captive giant chained
Whose breath came quickly as he strove and strained,
With hot sun beating pitilessly down,
Where dust lay thick upon the grass and trees
And birds sang only in rare startled spells,
I dreamed a dream of fragant-flowered leas,
Of murmuring waters blent with tinkling bells.

153

I, let me tell you frankly, am not one
To turn a deaf ear to a voice that's sweet.
Nor need its luring cadences repeat
Insistence, till insistence get that done
That gentle invitation tried in vain--
And so this dream of mine I dreamed no more
But, turning back on sordid care and pain
I sought the place--I knew it well of yore.

It is a nook to dream about, in faith,
A poet's idyl or a painter's fancy,
A charmed capital of necromancy,
Whose legended and ancient welcome saith:
"Who comes here, comes in peace, who leaves here, goes
With blessings rich and golden on his head.
Here dwell pale sister lily and queen rose;
Take, they are thine, and ring them garlanded."

It is a short hour's saunter from the old
And quiet village where the past still lives,
Where every noise and dying echo gives
A mellow ring as of our Age of Gold.
The silent streets are shadowy and green
With facing rows of venerable trees,
Where groups of happy children may be seen
With cheeks and eyes asparkling in the breeze.

And now and then a quaint old couple makes
Their feeble way adown the olden street;
Time's leaden weights hang heavily on their feet;
And faint and fair the light of Morning breaks.
Brusque childhood pauses curiously to take
Its unconcerned though still respectful look,
As one who cares not may at random make
An interested survey of a book.

Along the shaded street a soft sound floats,
The serene town's uninterrupted hum.
From fragrant fields balsamic odors come
Of wild-wood flowers, and ripening wheat and oats.
The softened sun-light lingeringly falls
On orchard-wall and bough of plum and peach,
Where low and sweet the loving song-bird calls,
Half-hid among the branches, out of reach.

A short hour's stroll along a winding way,
Now down a fresh and black-berry-briared lane,
Now through deep-shadowed woods and now again
Across the pregnant fields, the cottage lay
To which I came - - embowered like a shrine
For all Dame Nature's host to worship at - -
All-covered with a myriad-blossomed vine
That drapped its flower-like unasked blessings without stint.

That all was cleanly, beautiful and fair,
Betraying well its gentle owner's mind,
For not more grateful than is she refined
Was all the fragrance floating in the air.
Ah, me! that such a home-like gentle scene
Should startle memories of anguish past!
That Autumn's sombre doubting wistfulness at last
Should ever follow on the Summer's sheen!

The way last came meandering through a wood
Beneath tall oaks and chestnuts, here and there
Passing a melancholy pine whose rare
Sad countenance seemed but to brood and brood
On wrongs half-buried in a grave of fear,
Enduring still though bitterest at first - -
Snake-like it twisted till the end was near,
When suddenly on your sight the cottage burst.

Here then it was I met her face to face,
The dear companion of my boyish life,
The end of all my hope - - my little wife - -
My little all in those fair darling days.
Then love was but a name and life a lane
Studded with violets for our feet to press,
Leading straight on through many a wood and plain
To one high colored mansion called "Success" - -

Here then it was I met her, Miriam.
Here first by chance and after many years
Her frank, calm eyes scarce dimmed by pain or tears
Met mine in greeting, and a grateful calm
More deep and sweet and lasting than the glad
Free converse I had had with Nature's forms
Through all the pleasant saunter I had had - -
Fell on my troubled soul and calmed its storms.

Part II

"Full thirty years," she said. Full thirty years
Since she had seen me. Had it been so long,
Could the great tide of life have been so strong
That it had moved more rapid than our fears?
Or had we slept and dreamed of life and work
And busy haunts and pain and trouble sore,
Or bitter possibilities that lurk
Around, beneath, above, within us. More

Like a wild dream indeed it seems to be,
But yet, - - but yet - - this Miriam by my side,
This slender, graceful woman, weary-eyed,
Gray-haired and knowing all life's mystery!
Ah, Time indeed his will and way has had
And more than Time to make much more and worse
The mighty change that made her sweetness sad,
For suffering and sorrow have been hers.

156

O foolish faith that trusts aught in the past
Thinking and dreaming of a Present fled,
Luring in memories of a thing long-dead - -
Dry skins the adder Vanity hath cast - -
Accident rolls off blind Fancy's guarding-stone.
The body of the Past which long has lain
Sepulchred, has vanished - - all is gone,
Not e'en the ashes of dead trust remain.

Long years ago two little children went
Over the hill to school twice every day
And home returned to mingle in their play
The same blithe freedom child-like innocent.
The light of Heaven was in their happy faces,
The grace of health in every motion blent,
As hand in hand, they roamed the flowery places
And heard the bird songs, wondering what they meant.

When years had passed and he had come to know . . . .

On A Bundle Of Confederate Money

The time is out of joint. I should,
If things had gone a different way,
And all this dingy lot been good
Its printed promises to pay.

Have been a hateful moneyed man
And had no end of filthy pelf,
Instead of living as I can
And writing promises myself.

To My Last Year's Calendar

Now hath the year gone at last; and now
A young and princely follower maketh reign;
Sitteth a phraseless sterness on his brow
That bodeth of untempered vengeance ta'en.

This now regime, O constant friend, hath said
"All vassals faithful to the Old to death!"--
Thy crimes (would such were mine) are on thy head.
Such faith as thine no grace encountereth.

Harsh came the fell command in that first hour
The prince took sceptre from his hoary sire,
"Off with his head!" My faint hand lacketh power,
And so, farewell--I'll put thee in the fire.

My Old Colored Nurse

The dim light falls on the weary head
While my old nurse lies a-dreaming;
Her "children" are old (ah, me!) or dead
And she lies out-stretched on her simple bed
With the tears 'neath her eyelids gleaming.

She lies with the old gray head so still
It seems past reconciling.
She was always so proud, of a cheery will
Is it Harry or I or dear old Bill
Her fond old heart beguiling?

Dear Bill, poor boy, ah! he was the best
And he died like a soldier, fighting--
He went with a Southern heart in his breast
And his nurse's tears on the head she blessed--
Ah, nurse! your wrongs a-righting.

158

So the old nurse dreams with her smiles and tears
While the night is passing slowly,
And the old gray head with its unknown years
And the black-skinned forehead's wrinkled seers
I kiss as something holy.

My Daughter

By A Mother---

A saucy face with laughing grace,
Looked up with merry glee,
A roguish smile grew up meanwhile,
And flashed its gleams on me.

Her glossy curls my little girl's
Pure forehead strewed dishevelled;
Her little hand a magic wand;
A glist'ning sand-heap levelled.

Gay, sparkling, free, her bonnie, wee
Blue eyes with rippling laughter
Drew on my soul, beyond control,
When led to follow after.

* * * * * * * * * * * * *

A year (a day) rolled swift away.
Alas! all hope's bereft me.
A little shrine, (would that 'twere mine!)
Is all God's hand has left me.

159

This Sunday Morn

This Sunday morn my drowsy eyes
Drop closer as each minute flies;
The sound of exhortation notes
In measured cadence to me floats
And fills me with a vague surprise.
I'm sure my sleepy spirit tries
To be attentive, good, and wise.
But yet I dream of drifting boats
This Sunday Morn.

In through the open window gloats
The sun from fields of wheat and oats.
The green-clad splendor gleams, then dies,
Where dreamy mountain heights arise
I'll wake when sound the choiring throats
This Sunday Morn.

Smithsburg, Md.
Published but manuscript lost.

Genesis

High in the highest heaven rose-white within the blueness
The hands of all God's angels His flag of love unfurled
And o'er the dreaming ages burst forth a glorious newness
'Twas daylight in the world!

One Short Year

I know full well as do you all
In life, as nature, it is true
That distance weaves a magic thrall
And "lends enchantment to the view."

Across the plain of one short year
Our fancy, backward glancing, goes
And may-hap, moistened with a tear,
Conceals the thorn behind the rose.

And down our college years we scan
A vista glowing with a light
That marks to each his brother-man
In one eternal, simple right.

And by that light we see a joy
That beams upon each care-free face
That marked the triumph of the boy
Soon lifted to a sterner place.

Once more I tune my simple lyre,
Once more the quiet song you hear,
Once more I see the tender fire
I've seen not in this parting year.

I touch the silver chords again
For you its music never ends.
But ah! I sing a sadder strain
Than last year echoed to our friends.

The laugh, the jest have given place
To steady purpose and to thought.
We give "I will" a last embrace
And grapple with a stern "I ought"--

And yet I meant no "sadder" now
But "wiser" shall our poem be
And gladder, as on every brow
A quiet happiness I see.

I did not mean to cast a gloom
Upon this meeting of our band
My solid purpose did but loom
In vagueness--but you understand.

I sing a song of youth and love
And hope and purpose firmly set,
I hold my long-held hope above
That great shall be our guerdon yet.

We sing our battle psalm of life
With him who wrote "Excelsior"

And bravely enter on the strife
Within the endless corridor.

Then, class-mates, in that linked class
That parted here a year ago
Grip high the hearty quivering glass
And let the floods of friendship flow,

Drink to our youth, and drinking breathe
A prayer for manhood's ripened powers.
Drink, while this poem-crown I wreathe
And hide all sadness in its flowers.

A Youth

All alone a youth sits dreaming
Waking dreams oft dreamed before
In his weary eyes are gleaming
High Ambitions, Hope and more.

Oft his weary feet have faltered
Oft his fainting courage fled
Nearly had his purpose altered
Nearly had his strength been shed.

Only faith was young within him
Rallied by the soothing thought
That the angels gave to win him
Soft on angel-voices brought:
Choose the good and shun the ill
Time will all thy joy fulfill
Brave hearts win whate'er they will.

Ah! the doubts a youth possesses.
Ah! the shattered gods he tends.
Ah! the life of faith that presses
Onward to its tragic ends.

High ideals formed and broken
Lofty morals proven lies

162

Faith in noble efforts shaken
Winning skeptical replies.

Shrinking, trembling, stooping, fearing,
Knowing men and women false.
All the good as slaves appearing
In temptation's mighty thralls.

All that childhood's garden nourished,
Fading, dying everywhere.
Every simple flower that flourished
Fainting in a foetid air.

Purest springs made foul and deadening.
Finest bird notes harsh and dense,
Croaking out in chorus maddening
Death of truth and innocence.

Wonder not he yields, if tempted,
Wonder rather he is true --
No one ever is exempted
All must wade that river through.

What is life and all its longing,
What is love and all its woe,
Have the years deceived him thronging
Hope on hope -- to vanish so?

* * * * * * * * * * * * *

Ah, his mother's eyes come to him,
Trust is anchored in their depths,
Softly rings her love-song through him,
Softly all his sadness sleeps.

Mother love is all inspiring
Its unselfish purpose seeks,
With a tenderness untiring
Love her gentle presence speaks.

De Profundis

Sometimes (how often!) in my heart I feel
My life is like a coward sentinel
Who pales and trembles while he cries, "All's well,"
So little faith I have in aught of weal;
And at such times such sombre fancies steal
That life seems but a cracked and muffled bell
That beats such doleful music out 'twere well
To die, if dying could the dole repeal;
For man grows such a thing of art and show,
That more than ever is this world a stage,
And sweet simplicity we cannot know.
But could we shun the tawdry equipage,
Would aught of truer worth within us grow?
I know not -- nor does poet, priest or sage.

But yet I lose the weary weight of woe,
And catch the glimmer of that light of hope
That pierces through the darkness where I grope,
To guide me where the water-lilies grow
Of peace within the stream of faith, whose slow,
Eternal current stretches on where slope
Nepenthic meads of heavenly heliotrope,
Bounding the vision like a plain of snow.
Ah! Christ, the Only, enter all my soul;
Let Thy large Spirit come and be my own.
Teach me the way to gain a wise control
Of coward doubts that with my years have grown,
Help me to know my just environment,
And knowing, live; and living, be content.

Published in the "Lutheran Observer," January 14, 1887
Manuscript lost.

Lake Whitney Ice Skaters

Photo Courtesy of the New Haven Colony Historical Society